InterVarsity Press books

by James Emery White

Embracing the Mysterious God

Serious Times

The Prayer God Longs For

A MIND
for GOD

JAMES EMERY WHITE

An imprint of InterVarsity Press
Downers Grove, Illinois

InterVarsity Press
P.O. Box 1400, Downers Grove, IL 60515-1426
World Wide Web: www.ivpress.com
E-mail: email@ivpress.com

*InterVarsity Press® is the book-publishing division of InterVarsity Christian Fellowship/USA®, a student
movement active on campus at hundreds of universities, colleges and schools of nursing in the United States
of America, and a member movement of the International Fellowship of Evangelical Students.
For information about local and regional activities, write Public Relations Dept., InterVarsity Christian
Fellowship/USA, 6400 Schroeder Rd., P.O. Box 7895, Madison, WI 53707-7895, or visit the IVCF website
at <www.intervarsity.org>.*

All Scripture quotations, unless otherwise indicated, are taken from the Holy Bible, New International
Version®. NIV®. *Copyright ©1973, 1978, 1984 by International Bible Society. Used by permission of
Zondervan Publishing House. All rights reserved.*

Design: Cindy Kiple
Images: Siri Stafford/Getty Images

ISBN-10: 0-8308-3392-7
ISBN-13: 978-0-8308-3392-4

Printed in Canada ∞

Library of Congress Cataloging-in-Publication Data

White, James Emery, 1961-
A mind for God / James Emery White.
    p. cm.
Includes bibliographical references.
ISBN-13: 978-0-8308-3392-4 (cloth: alk. paper)
ISBN-10: 0-8308-3392-7 (cloth: alk. paper)
1. Thought and thinking—Religious aspects—Christianity. 2.
Christianity—Philosophy. I. Title.
BV4598.4.W45 2006
261—dc22

                                                                                        2006004127

P	17	16	15	14	13	12	11	10	9	8	7	6	5
Y	18	17	16	15	14	13	12	11	10	09	08		

Contents

Acknowledgments

*T*o my wife, Susan, who always makes every page of every book possible through her selflessness and support. To my four children—Rebecca, Rachel, Jonathan and Zachary—who already have minds far exceeding mine.

To the folks at InterVarsity Press, who can now only be called family. Cindy Bunch, who makes each book happen, and Jeff Crosby, who makes each book known, are kindred spirits and dear friends. Special thanks to Drew Blankman for stepping in during Cindy's sabbatical. Andrew Bronson, Krista Carnet and Brooke Nolen work tirelessly on each and every IVP title, and I enjoy every opportunity I have to thank them for their efforts with those bearing my name. To Bob Fryling, a simple thanks for sharing the larger vision.

To my assistant, Glynn Goble, goes continued gratitude; her constant cheer, servant's heart, selfless devotion and ongoing loyalty know no bounds. I am grateful to God for her ministry to my life.

Finally, a word of gratitude to the many men and women who have awakened the life of my mind: family and friends, authors and teachers, living and dead. In particular, I will forever be indebted to five men, all now with Christ, who challenged, stretched, invigorated and enlightened: Mortimer J. Adler, Walter Martin, Francis Schaeffer, C. S. Lewis and William L. Hendricks. Not the most likely of quintets to join forces, but God brought them together for me.

Introduction

A Mind for God

"I've preached too much, and studied too little."

BILLY GRAHAM

$\mathcal{A}$s I write, my oldest daughter is a freshman at one of the leading universities in the United States. In her first history course, her professor announced to the class that the entire historical record that Christianity is based on is untrue: Jesus never claimed to be the Messiah; none of his followers saw him as divine until centuries after his death; the Gospels are not first-hand accounts; Jesus was not a religious figure as much as he was a political one; there was never an intent to form any kind of "church"; there were dozens of "gospels," all of which were thought to be sacred by followers of the Jesus movement; and the four Gospels in the Bible today are riddled with discrepancies and errors.

In order to pass her first exam, she had to write that Jesus was born in Nazareth, not Bethlehem, deny Pauline authorship of 1 Timothy, and maintain that the four canonical Gospels are in complete disagreement on the major facts surrounding the death of Jesus—including when he was crucified, whether it was after the Passover or before, and whether Judas committed suicide.

In many ways, this was tame. A study of faculty members at U.S. colleges and universities found that 67 percent of faculty members either "strongly" or "somewhat" agree that homosexuality is as acceptable as heterosexuality. Eighty-four percent support abortion rights, and 75 percent support extramarital cohabitation. Fewer than a third described themselves as regular churchgoers.* When the Kansas Board of Education approved new science standards for teachers in public schools that questioned Charles Darwin's teachings on evolution (merely allowing the *idea* of "intelligent design" to be discussed), the director of the National Center for Science Education responded, "Those kids are in for a big shock when they go to college, because they're going to learn that what they had been taught by their teachers in high schools is a lot of rubbish."

Little wonder that cultural observers from Christian perspectives, such as Charles Colson, offer the following concern: "With the ever-increasing number of college professors who use their

*Notes can be found at the back of the book, beginning on page 115.

classrooms to indoctrinate students, rather than educate them, the views expressed and the lack of viewpoint diversity is deeply disturbing."

I will never forget my daughter calling me almost in tears over the statements made by the professor about her faith. Even with a firm worldview coupled with years of reading and instruction that enabled her to know how spurious the professor's claims were, she was emotionally shaken that her most deeply held values and convictions had been defamed and assaulted so vigorously. Even more, her heart was breaking over the three hundred other students in the class who sat passively, taking notes, accepting the professor's statements uncritically as fact.

Such volleys against faith come at us from every quarter and at every age: *The Da Vinci Code,* the bestselling novel to date for the twenty-first century, suggesting that Jesus was far from divine, sexually involved with Mary and bore a child; the most influential and popular film series in contemporary cultural ethos, *Star Wars,* propagating Eastern pantheistic thought; culture wars erupting over homosexuality and gay marriage, electoral politics, and the law; the debate surrounding evolution, intelligent design, and public education.

Far more often than not, our minds are not keeping up. It is a moment of both peril and promise; the peril is that when the public square is uniquely open to spirituality and hungry for visionary ideas, the mind of the Christian is often found empty, passive, and more reflective of the world at hand than the world to come. But the promise is that Christians can stride forward and engage the world at the point of its great need.

If the promise is fulfilled, it would not be the first time that the Christian mind has seized its moment.

In 1995 Thomas Cahill came out with the provocatively titled book *How the Irish Saved Civilization*. "Ireland," contended Cahill,

> had one moment of unblemished glory . . . as the Roman Empire fell, as all through Europe matted, unwashed barbarians descended on the Roman cities, looting artifacts and burning books, the Irish, who were just learning to read and write, took up the great labor of copying all of Western literature.

Then missionary-minded Irish monks brought what had been preserved on their isolated island back to the continent, refounding European civilization. And that, Cahill concludes, is how the Irish saved civilization.

But there is more at hand in Cahill's study than meets the eye. Beyond the loss of Latin literature and the development of the great national European literatures that an illiterate Europe would not have established, Cahill notes that something else would have perished in the West: "the habits of the mind that encourage thought."

Why would this matter?

Cahill continues his assessment: "And when Islam began its medieval expansion, it would have encountered scant resistance to its plans—just scattered tribes of animists, ready for a new identity." Without a robust mind to engage the onslaught—and a Christian one at that—the West would have been under the crescent instead of the cross.

Never before have the "habits of the mind" mattered more. As Winston Churchill presciently stated in his address to Harvard University in 1943: "The empires of the future will be empires of the mind." Oxford theologian Alister McGrath, reflecting on Churchill's address, notes that Churchill's point was that a great transition was taking place in Western culture, with immense implications for all who live in it. The powers of the new world would not be nation-states, as with empires past, but ideologies. It would now be ideas, not nations, that would captivate and conquer in the future. The starting point for the conquest of the world would now be the human mind.

But this time we may need more than the Irish to save us.

"We may talk of 'conquering' the world for Christ. But what sort of 'conquest' do we mean?" writes John Stott. "Not a victory by force of arms. . . . This is a battle of ideas." Yet there are surprisingly few warriors. Those who follow Christ have too often retreated into personal piety and good works, or as one BBC commentator I heard over the radio while jogging one morning in Oxford said, Christians have too often offered mere "feelings" and "philanthropy." Speaking specifically to the challenge from Islam, he added that what is needed was more "hard thinking" applied to the issues of the day.

What remains to be seen is whether there will be any hard thinkers to do it. The peril of our day is that when a Christian mind is most needed, Christians express little need for the mind, and as a result, even less resolve to develop it. There is even a sense that an undeveloped mind is more virtuous than one prepared for battle. Richard Hofstadter, in his Pulitzer Prize-winning book *Anti-Intellectualism in American Life,* identified "the evangelical spirit" as one of the prime sources of American anti-intellectualism. Hofstadter points out that for many Christians, humble ignorance is a far more noble human quality than a cultivated mind.

Such devaluation of the intellect is a recent development within the annals of Christian history. While Christians have long struggled with the role and place of reason, that the mind *itself* mattered has been without question.

Even the early church father Tertullian (c. A.D.160- c. 220), who had little use for philosophy and was famed for his statement "What indeed has Athens to do with Jerusalem?" never questioned the importance of the mind. Tertullian's conviction was that Greek philosophy had little to offer in terms of informing the contours of Christian thought, akin to the apostle Paul's quip to the Corinthian church that the foolishness of God is wiser than the wisdom of men (1 Corinthians 1:25). But Tertullian, as well as Paul, would have held any anti-intellectualism that celebrated an undeveloped mind in complete disdain.

Deep within the worldview of the biblical authors and equally within the minds of the earliest church fathers was the understanding that to be fully human is to *think*. To this day we call ourselves a race of Homo sapiens, which means "thinking beings." This is not simply a scientific classification; it is a *spiritual* one. We were made in God's image, and one of the most precious and noble dynamics within that image is the ability to think. It is simply one of the most sacred reflections of the divine image we were created in. It is also foundational to our interaction with God. As God himself implored through the prophet Isaiah: "Come now, let us reason together" (Isaiah 1:18).

This was certainly the conviction of Jesus, who made it clear that our minds are integral to life lived in relationship with God. When summarizing human devotion to God as involving heart, soul and strength, Jesus added *"and mind"* to the original wording of Deuteronomy, as if he wanted there to be no doubt that when contemplating the comprehensive nature of commitment and relationship with God our intellect would not be overlooked. The apostle Paul contended that our very *transformation* as Christians is dependent on whether our minds were engaged in an ongoing process of renewal in light of Christ (Romans 12:2-3).

All the more reason to be stunned by the words of Harry Blamires, a student of C. S. Lewis's at Oxford, who claimed that "there is no longer a Christian mind." A Christian ethic, a Christian practice, a Christian spirituality, yes—but not a Christian *mind*. More recently, historian Mark Noll concurred, suggesting that the scandal of the evangelical mind is that there is not much of an evangelical mind. "If evangelicals do not take seriously the larger world of the intellect, we say, in effect, that we want our minds to be shaped by the conventions of our modern universities and the assumptions of Madison Avenue, instead of by God and the servants of God."

And even if we do not lose our *own* minds, we will certainly lose the minds of others. This is the double-edged threat of our day; apart from a Christian mind we will either be taken captive by the myriad of worldviews contending for our attention, or we will fail to make the Christian voice heard and considered above the din. Either way, we either begin to think or lose the fight.

That is the purpose of this small book: *thinking Christianly.* While short in length, it sketches out a very large challenge and investment: to develop our minds in light of a biblical worldview that is then used to think Christianly about the world. From this we will be able as Christians to respond to the culture we live in and help the culture respond to the Christ we follow. This was the clarion call of the apostle Paul, who reminded the Corinthian church that "we do not wage war as the world does. . . . We demolish arguments and every pretension that sets itself up against the knowledge of God, and we take captive every thought to make it obedient to Christ" (2 Corinthians 10:3, 5).

The Christian Mind

"Most Christians would rather die than think; in fact they do."

BERTRAND RUSSELL

*O*ne summer while studying at Oxford University in England, I was invited to a reception for visiting students. Within the first five minutes, I found myself in conversation with two women, one from Florida and the other from California. After exchanging the usual pleasantries, I was asked what I did for a living.

I told them that I was the pastor of a church.

The woman from Florida seemed primed for the moment. "Well, I'm glad somebody like you is at a place like this so that you can give people the truth. You know, the *real* story. Why don't more ministers do that?"

"Well," I said, "I'm not sure I know what you're talking about."

"You know, all of that stuff about Jesus having died on a cross, resurrected on the third day and all the miracles. I mean, he

never died like that. In fact, he lived a long, full life, got married
and had kids.

"Oh, really?" I said.

"Don't you believe that?" She was incredulous.

I had just met this woman and didn't want to immediately
launch into a debate with her—it was, after all, such a pleasant English afternoon—but this was a bit much. I searched for the least in-
flammatory response I could think of: "I'm sure there are those who
might agree with you, but I confess that I am not one of them."

"You mean you believe all of that stuff in the Bible?"

"Yes," I replied.

"You mean, like the virgin birth?"

"Yes," I said.

You could see it written all over her face. Here was a seemingly
intelligent man studying at Oxford who says he believes the Bible.
There was, to her eyes, something terribly wrong with this picture.

Our conversation went on in earnest but with a fascinating
twist. While the woman from Florida continued to ask questions
and raise objections, her friend from California joined with me to
try to explain that perhaps some of the sources for her reconstruc-
tion of Jesus and the Christian faith were less than sound.

Impressed by her perspective, I said to my new ally, "So would
you consider yourself a Christian?"

"No," she said. "I'm open to it, but would still consider myself
something of a seeker."

Then to my surprise, the woman with whom I'd been debating said, "Well, I would certainly consider *myself* a Christian."

Such conversations raise a foundational question: What does it mean for a mind to be Christian? In that English garden, behind Christ Church Cathedral in Oxford, a woman who was not a follower of Christ was more orthodox and biblical (and informed) in her thinking than one who professed an allegiance to Christ. Is a Christian mind something that can be detailed? Of course. This is one of the principal tasks of the queen of the sciences, Christian theology. As I teach my seminary students, one of the primary goals of Christian theology is to determine what is—and what is not—orthodoxy. There is right thinking, and there is wrong thinking. *Wrong* thinking, in theological terms, is called heresy.

And there is much heresy.

The National Study of Youth and Religion, conducted from 2001 to 2005 and perhaps the largest research project on the religious and spiritual lives of American adolescents, cataloged the demise of a Christian worldview *among Christians*. While the vast majority of U.S. teenagers identified themselves as Christian, the "language, and therefore experience, of Trinity, holiness, sin, grace, justification, sanctification, church, Eucharist, and heaven and hell appear, among most Christian teenagers in the United States, . . . to be supplanted by the language of happiness, niceness, and an earned heavenly reward."

Principal investigator Christian Smith writes, "It is not so much that U.S. Christianity is being secularized. Rather more subtly, Christianity is either degenerating into a pathetic version of itself or, more significantly, Christianity is actively being colonized and displaced by a quite different religious faith."

Smith and his colleagues call this new faith "Moralistic Therapeutic Deism," a belief system that embraces the existence of a God who demands little more than to be "nice," with the central goal of life to be happy and feel good about oneself. God is not particularly needed in daily life except to resolve various problems that might come our way (think "Divine Butler" or "Cosmic Therapist"). And regardless of religious convictions, beliefs or commitments, good people go to heaven when they die.

This is *not* a Christian mind based on a biblical worldview.

So what is?

A Christian mind is not simply thinking done by those who consider themselves Christians. Jesus confronted Peter and bluntly informed him, "Away with you, Satan. . . . You think as men think, not as God thinks" (Matthew 16:23 NEB). It is not simply thinking about Christian *things,* such as reflecting on Jesus or grace or the nature of the church. Also it should not be confused with attempting to adopt a Christian perspective on every issue. Even if such perspectives were possible, they would flow *from* a Christian mind—they would not constitute a Christian mind in and of themselves.

Instead, Os Guinness wisely writes that "thinking Christianly is thinking by Christians about anything and everything in a consistently Christian way—in a manner that is shaped, directed, and restrained by the truth of God's Word and God's Spirit." The Christian faith is not simply a defined worldview but a faith which claims to be based on *revelation.* Unlike a political system or body of humanly produced legislation, the Christian faith contends that God has chosen to reveal himself and truth about himself through Scripture and supremely in Christ that could not otherwise be known. The very meaning of the word "revelation" from the Latin *revelatio,* is to "draw back the curtain," to reveal to us that which would have remained hidden had God not chosen to engage in the act of revelation.

There is then a great divide when it comes to how we approach the very act of thinking. The nature of this divide should not be underestimated, for it has separated humanity from the dawn of civilization. Its distinctive wedge has shaped discourse and debate, philosophy and reason, science and commerce. Yet as broad as the divide may be, the essence of the chasm is simple: *there is either something outside of ourselves that we must take into account or there is not.*

The *Christian* mind is a mind that operates under the belief that there *is* something outside of ourselves that we must take into account. There *is* a God, a God, as Francis Schaeffer said, who is not only there but is not silent. Thinking in light of God's existence and his self-revelation is what it means to have a Christian mind. It is seeing the world in light of faith. Or it is being a "Christian Realist," as Flannery O'Connor would refer to herself, which reflected her conviction that she lived in the presence of certain theological truths, such as the doctrine of creation, the fall and redemption. These were not simply matters of subjective belief; they were part of the nature of reality, as solid as the laws of physics.

For O'Connor the Christian faith could not be something without substance, without meaning, without an absolute rooting in reality. In "Novelist and Believer" she wrote:

> It makes a great difference to the look of a novel whether its author believes that the world came late into being and continues to come by a creative act of God, or whether he believes that the world and ourselves are the product of a cosmic accident. It makes a great difference to his novel whether he believes that we are created in God's image, or whether he believes we create God in our own. It makes a great difference whether he believes that our wills are free, or bound like those of other animals.

This, then, is the stark divide between a Christian mind and what might best be called a naturalistic mind, meaning a mind that, in terms of truth and meaning, accepts nothing outside of the natural realm. The Christian mind believes that God is on the loose; a naturalistic mind does not. A Christian mind believes this God brought forth truth and order, purpose and authority into the created cosmos; the naturalistic mind believes there is no truth, no authority outside of ourselves and the naturalistic processes of the universe. This is the great divide, and its nature is what sets the Christian mind apart from all others.

It is also what presents the great challenge to the Christian mind from the modern world.

The Cultural Mind

"Our minds are as the days are, dark or bright."

HOMER

*I*n his provocatively titled book *From Darwin to Hitler,* historian Richard Weikart examines the revolutionary impact Darwinism had on the ethics and morality of social thinkers in Nazi Germany. Believing that Darwinism had overturned any sense of the sanctity of human life, an evolutionary "fitness" (especially in terms of intelligence and health) became the highest arbiter of morality for the Nazis. Weikart concludes that Darwinism played a strategic role not only in the rise of eugenics but also in the rise of euthanasia, infanticide, abortion and racial extermination—all ultimately embraced by the Nazis.

The contention that Hitler built his views on Darwinian principles raises one of the most important truths a mind can comprehend: *Ideas have consequences.* This is what Richard Weaver titled his seminal work, asserting that the catastrophes of our age are the product not of necessity but of choice. Increasingly, the basis of that choice is a worldview divorced from spiritual moorings. The great Russian novelist Aleksandr Solzhenitsyn, speaking of his country's spiritual demise, concurred, saying, "If I were asked today to formulate as concisely as possible the main cause of the ruinous Revolution that swallowed up some sixty million of our people, I could not put it more bluntly than to repeat: 'Men have forgotten God; that's why all this has happened.' " The solution, Weaver contends, is the right use of reason, which entails a recognition of absolute reality and a recognition that ideas—like actions—have consequences.

But this is not a conviction that shapes our world.

Though a 2004 survey of religion and politics sponsored by the Pew Forum on Religion and Public Life found only 7.5 percent of the American population categorized themselves as "secularists," columnist David Klinghoffer maintains that those embracing secularism far exceed the 7.5 percent figure, as many individuals who identify nominally as Jews or Christians are, in fact, devout secularists. Perhaps even more decisive is to consider the secularized subculture currently resting at the top of the American educational system, the media of mass communication and the upper echelons of the legal system. These are the epicenters of culture and the means by which values and ideas come into being and are disseminated. While their forces may be "relatively thin on the ground," sociologist Peter Berger observes, "they are very influential, as they control the institutions that provide the 'official' definitions of reality." Berger quips, "If India is the most religious country on our planet, and Sweden is the least religious, America is a land of Indians ruled by Swedes." So a country like the United States is clearly secularized politically, and arguably intellectually; it just may take a while for it to get to the "man on the street."

It should be noted that by secularism I do not mean atheism, which is, as Alister McGrath has written, entering into its twilight as an idea. Atheism is neither at the heart of the secular religion nor the principal challenge to Christian faith. The heart of the secular religion is moral relativism, a *functional* atheism, if you will, which holds that what is moral is dictated by a particular situation in light of a particular culture or social location. With moral relativism, moral values become a matter of personal opinion or private judgment rather than something grounded in objective truth.

But few see this as the great challenge facing the Christian faith. An online poll conducted by AOL soon after the selection of Cardinal Joseph Ratzinger to be the next pope revealed what people perceived as Pope Benedict XVI's greatest challenges. "Sanctity of life" issues, such as cloning or stem cells, came in first, followed by the priest shortage. Distant on the list was the rise of secularism.

Fortunately, the new pope is not driven by polls, exhibiting a sound awareness of secularism's threat and wisely discerning that "sanctity of life" issues and the priest shortage are the symptoms of secularism's rise. Benedict XVI has had a courtside seat to secularism's deadly effects in Western Europe and specifically his German homeland. Fewer than one of every ten Germans worships even once a month, and a majority of Germans and other Northern Europeans confess that God does not matter to them at all (which accounts for the absence of any reference to God in the draft of the proposed European constitution).

Little wonder that in Ratzinger's pre-election sermon to his fellow cardinals he made the following declaration: "We are moving toward a dictatorship of relativism . . . that recognizes nothing definite and leaves only one's ego and desires as the final measure." John Paul II began his papacy with the cry "Be not afraid!" Benedict XVI seemed to initiate his pontificate differently: "Be afraid. Be very, very afraid." And we should be. But more than afraid, we should be aware; if the war we wage is one of ideas, we must be aware of those ideas arrayed against us.

The mind for God faces a cultural challenge: the god of this world—who is not without intellectual forces, which he arrays against the kingdom. Within this assault are four major ideas, each of which is critical to understand.

MORAL RELATIVISM

The first idea within our culture that is in direct opposition to a biblical worldview is that of moral relativism. The basic idea of moral relativism is: What is true for you is true for you, and what is true for me is true for me. What is moral is dictated by a particular situation in light of a particular culture or social location. Moral values become a matter of personal opinion or private judgment rather than something grounded in objective truth.

This is so entrenched in Western culture that Allan Bloom, reflecting on his role as a university educator, maintains that there "is one thing a professor can be absolutely certain of. Almost every student entering the university believes, or says he believes, that truth is relative." Much of this has led to a changing view of reality itself, based on the growing sense that no one can be truly objective. You cannot stand outside of your own context—including experiences, biases and the historical-cultural current—and be free to make an unconditioned observation. More than the sentiment "That's your opinion," the idea is that *everything* is opinion. This does not mean that there is not a reality "out there," just that all of our "stories" about what is "out there" are the products of individual, highly subjective minds engaging "what is." So reality is little more than what we as individuals perceive it to be.

Because truth is considered to be relative, existing only in the realm of our private opinions and preferences, matters of faith are increasingly rejected in the public sphere. Far more than being perceived as showing poor form, explicit talk of faith has been banished from the wider public agenda. As historian and educator Page Smith once sarcastically observed, in our day, "God is not a proper topic for conversation, but 'lesbian politics' is." Unless it becomes politically expedient, then "God" is resurrected and bandied about as if a part of one's resume (as has become the rage of late). Yet this is far from a defined God, meaning the One who has revealed himself and truth about himself. Spirituality and religion may be "in"; transcendent truth, which is exclusive by its very nature and claims lordship over an entire life, is not.

So while Christianity used to be rejected by Enlightenment intellectuals because they thought its central beliefs had been disproven by science or philosophy, today it is disqualified on the grounds that it argues for a truth that is unchanging and universal. A particular faith used to be wrong on the basis of what was perceived to be truth; now a faith is wrong for claiming there *is* truth. As Allen Bloom has wryly noted, "The true believer is the real danger."

AUTONOMOUS INDIVIDUALISM

A second idea coursing through the currents of culture is that of autonomous individualism.

To be autonomous is to be independent. Autonomous individualism maintains that each person is independent in terms of destiny and accountability. Ultimate moral authority is *self*-generated. In the end, we answer to no one but ourselves, for we are truly on our own. Our choices are ours alone, determined by our personal pleasure, and not by any higher moral authority.

As opposed to the Christian idea, famously articulated by Dutch leader Abraham Kuyper, that there is not an inch of any sphere of our lives that Christ does not declare "Mine!" current thinking would respond "How dare you!" Or even more to the point, "Who do you think you are?" The answer Christ would give, of course, is "God," but that would be the point of contention. As the French existentialist philosopher Jean Paul Sartre contended, "Man is the being whose project is to be God."

NARCISSISTIC HEDONISM

A third idea the Christian worldview must contend with is narcissistic hedonism.

In Greek mythology, Narcissus is the character that, on seeing his reflection in the water, becomes so enamored with himself that he devotes the rest of his life to his own reflection. From this we get the term *narcissism,* signifying a preoccupation with self. The value of narcissistic hedonism is the classic "I, me, mine" mentality that places personal pleasure and fulfillment at the forefront of concerns.

Or as Francis Schaeffer maintained throughout his writings, the ultimate ethic of the day seems to be the pursuit of personal peace and individual affluence. In agreement with Schaeffer's conclusion, the noted cultural historian Christopher Lasch christened ours "the culture of narcissism," determining that the current taste is for individual therapy instead of religion. The quest for personal well-being, health and psychic security has replaced the older hunger for personal salvation.

This runs deeper than mere self-gratification. Narcissism has become a guiding worldview. Stanley Grenz observed that Anselm's famed dictum "I believe in order that I may understand" was altered by the Enlightenment to become "I believe what I can understand." The modern twist goes further, becoming "I believe when I understand that it helps me." This puts the idea that rests at the heart of the Christian faith—that of self-sacrifice—in more than opposition to the culture. The modern world can barely fathom its embrace.

REDUCTIVE NATURALISM

Gerard Piel, founder and publisher of *Scientific American* magazine, has argued that when historians examine Western civilization of the twentieth century, it will be deemed the "age of science." But not just any kind of science; ours will be the age of *naturalism,* the idea that nature is "all that is." This is the fourth idea rooted in our culture. Naturalism holds that life is accidental. There is nothing beyond ourselves that will ever bring order, reason or explanation.

Reductive naturalism states that all that can be known within nature is that which can be empirically verified. What is real is only that which can be seen, tasted, heard, smelled or touched and then *verified,* meaning able to be replicated through experimentation. Knowledge is "reduced" to this level of knowing. If it cannot be examined in a tangible, scientific manner, it is not simply unknowable but meaningless.

Even dangerous.

As astronomer Carl Sagan argued in his final work, the goal is to rid ourselves of a "demon-haunted" world, meaning anything that would challenge the rule of science and technology as the ultimate arbiter of truth and reality, for there is no other truth or reality to embrace. So we do not simply have science but *scientism*—the deification of scientific methods and results as religion.

MODERNITY'S WAKE

For the Christian mind, understanding the world we live in is decisive on two fronts. First, we need to be aware of how such worldviews might be living in *us*. Is our thinking informed and directed by the authority of Scripture and the leading of the Holy Spirit, or have we succumbed to the subtle temptation of moral relativism? Do we mark our years by dedication to God and his eternal purposes, or do we strip our lives of any sense of calling and answer only to the voice of an autonomous individualism? Do we live in light of the great redemptive drama, selflessly giving ourselves to the advance of the kingdom and the building of the church, or do we find ourselves drifting into a narcissistic hedonism that makes all spiritual alignments a consumer affair? Do we view the world through a materialistic lens, or do we see a God who not only created but who, through his providence, continues to oversee that creation?

Second, we need to understand how the world affects those around us who we will engage for Christ, not simply in terms of intellectual challenge but also in terms of unmet needs. How might we begin to live and speak and act and serve in ways that might intersect with their deepest questions and longings?

And the world has left much unmet.

The *trauma* of our world is that the secular worldview, rooted in naturalism, has failed to deliver on its promises. Rather than enhancing personal satisfaction and fulfillment, we live in a moral and spiritual wasteland. *Moral relativism* has led to a crisis in values; we find ourselves needing values but not having them, and divorced from any means of finding them. *Autonomous individualism* has led to a lack of vision; there is nothing calling us upward to be more than we are beyond our selves. *Narcissistic hedonism* has fostered empty souls; anyone who has followed its ever-deadening trail knows how hollow its entreaties are. And of course *reductive naturalism* has proven inadequate for human experience; we intuitively know that there is more to reality than what our five senses can verify, and we long to find that which is beyond ourselves.

But do Christians have anything to offer the world that it does not already have? Are we able to present Christ so clearly that non-Christians understand he alone is able to intersect the deepest needs of their life?

Not unless we forge our minds on the anvil of development. And the rest of this book is dedicated to examining just what that might look like.

T H R E E

The Library as Armory

"When you come, bring . . . my scrolls, especially the parchments."

A POSTLE P AUL TO T IMOTHY

I love to read. As a young boy I can remember devouring Ellery Queen mysteries on long vacation drives, taking a hot bath and reading *The Long Winter* by Laura Ingalls Wilder, curling up in the bay window of a local library, as rain cascaded down the glass, with a harrowing tale of Blackbeard the Pirate. I still have the copy of Roald Dahl's *Charlie and the Chocolate Factory,* worn from countless readings, given to me on my twelfth birthday by my grandmother. For me, the perfect day is one with a sky full of dark and heavy clouds, promising a furious rain storm or inches of snow, with a fire in the fireplace and a book by my side waiting to be explored.

My love of reading as a boy grew into something altogether different when I became a follower of Christ in college. Reading took on an urgency that it had never held before. Attending a secular university as a new Christian was not an easy task. I was surrounded by very bright people who were not Christ-followers and were eager to explain why. To hold on to my faith, much less contend for it, would demand fulfilling the Bible's clear and commanding exhortation to "always be prepared to give an answer to everyone who asks you to give the reason for the hope that you have" (1 Peter 3:15). I knew I had to out-think those who were challenging my faith; and to out-think them, I knew I had to out-read them. From this, reading moved from mere pleasure to real purpose. No longer did it matter whether I enjoyed reading; it had become *essential*.

From reading alone could I gain a sense of the currents shaping the world; from reading alone could I understand the prevailing worldviews assailing Christianity; from reading alone could I place myself in the vanguard of taking the Word of God to the word of the world. Reading would fill my mind with virtually limitless knowledge, instruction and insight, and it would exercise my mind and force it to break through barriers of stagnancy.

So I read the existentialist philosophers, such as Camus and Sartre. I read the great Greek thinkers, such as Plato and Aristotle. I delved into history, literature and science. I read the plays of Ibsen and Beckett. I was purposeful in my approach because I was on a mission to prepare my mind to not simply understand the ideas of the world but to engage the ideas of the world. And not simply to challenge others but to find everywhere God's truth existed—for all truth is God's truth, and the presence of that truth is the beginning of dialogue and redemption. I was not the first to hold to this conviction. As a monk in Normandy wrote in 1170: "A monastery without a library *[sine armario]* is like a castle without an armory *[sine armamentario]*. Our library is our armory." This was certainly the conviction of the apostle Paul, who even from his prison cell in Rome implored Timothy to be sure to bring him his books (2 Timothy 4:13).

Yet according to the comprehensive "Reading at Risk" report (2002) from the National Endowment of the Arts, for the first time in modern history, less than half of the adult population now reads literature, reflecting a larger decline in all other sorts of reading— a rate of decline that is accelerating, particularly among the young.

The report cataloged a massive cultural shift toward electronic media for not only entertainment but also information, which can make reading seem superfluous. Such a shift comes at great cost, for much is lost when reading is discarded—much more than the · knowledge that might have been gained through the act of reading itself. Reading a book requires a degree of engagement, of active attention, that enlivens and expands the mind. Electronic media makes far fewer demands; it breeds passive participation, fosters shorter attention spans and creates the demands for immediate gratification. The report went on to note that the diminishing print culture brings a diminished capacity for focused attention and contemplation that makes complex communications and insights possible. In the end, it can lead us to forgo the practice of active learning altogether.

As a result, reading is the *foundation* for intellectual development.

My wife was an elementary education major in college and chose to homeschool each of our four children through to the eighth grade. While we partnered on this, my part was, to say the least, secondary. My wife guided each of our four children to an education that served them admirably throughout high school and college, and the heart of her curriculum was reading. Homeschooling is a challenging and arduous task. When nothing went as planned (e.g., math assignments left uncompleted, science projects remained undone), Susan would wearily collapse into a chair at the end of the day and say, "Well, at least they read. If I can just get them to read, everything else will fall into place." And she was right. It would, and it did. The national campaign in the United States that touted reading as "fundamental" was one of the truest campaigns ever launched through the media.

Yet there is far more that reading brings into our life. It prepares us to *think,* for it is reading which allows us to understand and interpret the *events* of our day. The Christian mind cannot simply absorb the news; it must consider the news in light of God's purposes in the world. How should we think about what is happening? What does it mean? What should our response be? Susan Wise Bauer suggests that when you hear the morning news, you may find out that a suicide bomber has just devastated a restaurant on the West Bank. This is nothing but information—a collection of facts—gained passively, without exertion and taken at face value. "What a tragedy," we might add. "But in order to be enlightened about the suicide bombers on the West Bank," Bauer writes, "you must read seriously: history, theology, politics." Information alone simply washes over us, Bauer adds, without leaving its traces behind. Or, one might add, its implications. "Wrestling with truth," she concludes, "marks us forever."

The critical importance of reading reminds me of something I came across long ago—so long that the author now escapes me. But I recall it was a lament for a book never read. The loss of pages never turned, covers never opened, words never seen. A single book can deepen your understanding, expand your vision, sensitize your spirit, deepen your soul, ignite your imagination, stir your passions and widen your wisdom. There truly can be mourning for a book never read—mourning for the loss of what our lives could have held and could have accomplished.

CHOOSING TO READ

How can we become active readers in the midst of the frantic pace of our lives? It is tempting to view the act of sitting down with a book—much less many books—as a luxury afforded those with unique schedules or privileged positions in life. In truth, it is available to us all. It is simply a matter of choice or, perhaps more accurately, a series of choices.

To read, you must first *position* yourself to read. I have learned to keep books around me. When I travel, when I take my car to have the oil changed, when I pick my children up from school, when I go to the doctor's office, I bring a book, journal or magazine. If you were to look around my home, you would see stacks of books everywhere: on the tables by the side of beds, on the floor by chairs.

But this reflects a deeper decision in relation to reading. Having a book at hand is only of use if I choose to spend available time reading it. Key to that choice is the word *available*. I once heard Jim Collins, known best as the author of business titles, comment that we do not need to make more "to do" lists but rather a few "stop doing" lists. I know that in my life the great opposition to reading is what I allow to fill my time *instead* of reading. To say we have no time to read is not really true; we have simply chosen to use our time for other things or have allowed our time to be filled to the exclusion of reading.

And there is little doubt what offers the greatest temptation.

According to a 1997 study reported in the *New York Times*, the average person in America spent about 1,100 hours a year watching broadcast TV, an additional 500 hours watching cable TV and 300 hours listening to music. Only 100 hours were spent reading. Imagine what a repeat of this now-dated study would find in light of the time spent on the Internet. Neil Postman noted that the great fear of George Orwell, as conveyed in his novel *1984,* was of a day when there might be those who would ban books. Aldous Huxley's portrait of the future in *Brave New World* was more prescient; Huxley feared that there would be no reason to ban a book, for there would be no one who wanted to read one.

Recently my family and I visited Disney World in Orlando, Florida. There for a week, we developed a pattern of going to the parks early in the morning, coming back to the hotel for a mid-afternoon break and then going back out for the evening. One day, during one of the afternoons back at the hotel, we were sitting in the atrium around a table doing what seemed normal to us as a family.

We were reading.

My oldest daughter was tearing through the latest installment of Harry Potter in order to pass it on to her siblings; my other daughter was soldiering her way through Dostoevsky's *The Brothers Karamazov;* my oldest son was reading—again—Tolkien's trilogy *The Lord of the Rings;* and my youngest son was laughing uproariously over some unfortunate event conceived by Lemony Snicket.

I had my own stack of books beside me, as if they were a mound of pastries from which I had yet to choose which one to eat first. A history by David McCullough, I believe, finally won. My wife, bless her soul, was actually reading one of her husband's books. Martyrs still exist.

A woman walked over to our table, openly marveling at seeing six people—and particularly four children—*reading.* She said it was a wonderful sight and wondered how we did it. I remember thinking that we didn't do anything—we genuinely enjoyed reading. But there was something that caused my children to love a book. It started by doing what my mother did—talking about books like they were truly a pleasure. Then, throughout their lives, we modeled a life that read.

But another thought entered my mind. What led us to read that day? The same thing that had led us to read a thousand days before. On that day, upon returning to the hotel room, the TV went on just like it would in your family. But then Susan and I instinctively said to our kids, "Why don't you get a book and read instead? Come on, let's go out together and sit by a table and read." So we did.

But first, the choice had to be made.

WHAT TO READ

But *what* should we read? It is one thing to be widely read, but something altogether different to be *well* read. The difference is important.

When it comes to the actual books we open, it is very essential to be selective. As Arthur Schopenhauer once suggested, "If a man wants to read good books, he must make a point of avoiding bad ones; for life is short, and time and energy limited." Richard Weaver observes that it may be doubted whether one person in three draws what may be correctly termed "knowledge" from his freely chosen reading matter.

This is not a matter of avoiding what is often termed "beach reads"—those books that are light, frivolous page-turners. Just as exercise can and should involve play, sport, and recreation, so reading should involve fun and fantasy, escape and entertainment. But if this is all that reading holds for us, our minds will quickly become the equivalent of a body that eats only fast food. In the 2004 documentary film *Super Size Me,* a mere thirty days of such diet resulted in weight gain of twenty-five pounds, chest pains, liver problems and trouble breathing. Imagine what month after month and year after year of feeding our *minds* such a diet would produce.

So what are the "good" books? Where is "knowledge" gained? Robert Maynard Hutchins observes, "Until lately the West has regarded it as self-evident that the road to education lay through the great books." And what are the great books? "There never was very much doubt in anybody's mind about which the masterpieces were," writes Hutchins. "They were the books that had endured and that the common voice of mankind called the finest creations, in writing, of the Western mind." The great books are those writings that have most shaped history and culture, civilization and science, politics and economics. They prompt us to think about the great issues of life. C. S. Lewis simply called them the "old" books.

Actual collections of such writings have been attempted. Along with Mortimer Adler, Hutchins compiled a set of "Great Books" that spanned Homer to Freud, covering more than twenty-five centuries, including the works of Plato and Aristotle, Virgil and Augustine, Shakespeare and Pascal, Locke and Rousseau, Kant and Hegel, Darwin and Dostoevsky. Charles W. Eliot, who served as president of Harvard for forty years, dreamed of a five-foot shelf of books that would provide an education to anyone who would spend even fifteen minutes a day reading them. His vision took form when he became the editor of the fifty-volume *Harvard Classics* (1909).

Critiques can be made of such reading programs, both in scope and intent, but at least they propel the reader into what Hutchins calls the "Great Conversation."[†] Or as René Descartes would suggest, the reading of such books is like a conversation with the noblest men of past centuries, "nay a carefully studied conversation, in which they reveal to us none but the best of their thoughts." Lewis went further, arguing that the old books were needed to confront our current ages perspective. "Every age has its own outlook," Lewis contended. "It is specially good at seeing certain truths and specially liable to make certain mistakes. We all, therefore, need the books that will correct the characteristic mistakes of our own period. And that means the old books."

Lewis was right. As the author of Ecclesiastes noted, there is very little that is new under the sun. The ancient heresy of Gnosticism, which holds to "secret" knowledge through a spiritual enlighten-

---

[†]In the first appendix to this volume, I offer my own suggested list of books for the great conversation.

ment and emphasizes the spiritual over the material, rears its head on an ongoing basis. The voice of Pelagius continues to echo down the centuries, suggesting that we must, or at least can, do something to earn our salvation. And much within postmodernism is simply the philosophy of Friedrich Nietzsche coming into his own.

If every generation of Christians faces these ideas as if for the first time, the damage will be incalculable. The old phrase "fool me once, shame on you; fool me twice, shame on me" rings true. Not only will vast amounts of time and resources be wasted grappling with what Christians have already addressed, but large numbers of casualties will be tallied on both sides; Christians who fall prey to such thinking and non-Christians who might have been receptive to the gospel will be subject to distortions that confuse their thinking and ability to respond to the gospel.

Our tendency, of course, is not to read the old books at all, or at least to do no more than read books *about* the old books. More often than not it is because we determine in advance that they are beyond us, are irrelevant or would be dry, dull reading. The wonderful surprise is how seldom this is true. Some might take more effort than others, but that *is* the point—to exercise the mind. We accept that getting into physical shape will take determination, will power and sweat. The mind demands no less yet offers so much more.

THE GREAT BOOK

Of course, the foundation of the Christian mind is *the* great book—the Bible. It is God's revelation to us, imparting knowledge that cannot be known apart from its revelation. The Bible alone is "living and active. Sharper than any double-edged sword, it penetrates even to dividing soul and spirit, joints and marrow; it judges the thoughts and attitudes of the heart" (Hebrews 4:12).

As one would expect, the Bible is not to be read like any other book. More than concentrated study of the Scriptures is called for; this is a book to be *obeyed.* Other books are to be engaged, understood and evaluated as to the truth and wisdom, place and purpose of their contents. The Bible must also be engaged and understood, but not for the purpose of determining whether we should take it into consideration. The Bible alone calls for complete and utter submission of life and thought. As New Testament scholar N. T. Wright observes, "The Christian is prepared to say, 'I don't like the sound of this, but golly, if this is what it really means, I'm going to have to pray for grace and strength to get that into my heart and be shaped by it.'"

Sadly, very few read the Bible, as Gordon Fee titled one of his books, "for all that it's worth." As I have observed as both pastor and educator, there are many ways people read the Bible. There are "service" readers, those who engage the Bible when it is presented during a weekend service, and that is all. Then there are devotional readers who take bite-size bits of Scripture through secondary conduits (devotional magazines or books). This goes light-years beyond the "service" reader because it encourages reflection on a text, but it is far from the feast the Scriptures offer and the mind needs. What is required is studious reading: an open Bible, a dictionary and concordance nearby, and time to reflect on what the psalmist described as "a lamp to my feet and a light for my path" (Psalm 119:105). This is the foundation of the Christian mind. A biblical worldview—a view of the world informed and shaped by the Bible—has always marked the most developed and formidable of Christian minds.

Consider Augustine. In *Loving God,* Charles Colson recalls how Augustine—brilliant, learned and handsome—held one of the most prestigious and enviable professorships in Italy. When he spoke, he was overwhelmingly persuasive. Few considered themselves his equal. Although he had a Christian mother and was personally intrigued by the Christian faith, Augustine lived a life distant from God. He was torn about how best to live; he was engaged to be married, yet had a mistress and an illegitimate child. In fact, he had many mistresses. Sex was necessary for him, he said, for he had no power to resist his natural desires. On the other hand, he was riddled with guilt, even from the time he stole fruit from a neighbor's pear tree with a gang of youthful rowdies.

But change was afoot in Augustine's heart. The great philosophers, such as Plato, had convinced Augustine that there was more to the world than what could be seen, tasted, touched, heard or smelled. Things beyond his own senses could be real. Then Augustine encountered Ambrose, a Christian pastor in Milan. In Ambrose, Augustine found a speaker equal to his own rhetorical skills. But Ambrose had more than verbal ability—Augustine was intrigued with what Ambrose was *saying*.

Augustine had tried reading the Scriptures as a teenager but was not impressed. At the time he had been in love with beautiful language, and the language of Scripture seemed dull and plain. But years had passed since then. Under Ambrose's influence, the simplicity of Scripture began to sound *profound*.

One evening he sat in his garden, utterly silent in the stillness of the summer heat. But inside his heart, a storm raged. Confusion over his life built up until finally it seemed as if his chest would burst. He threw himself under a fig tree, unable to stop sobbing.

Then . . . a voice.

A childish, piping voice seemed to come from a nearby house. It chanted over and over, "Take up and read. Take up and read. Take up and read."

Were the words for him?

"Read what?" Augustine shouted into the sky.

Then he glanced around him, and there, lying nearby, were the letters of the apostle Paul from the New Testament. *Was he to take up the Scriptures and read?*

He snatched up the book and began reading where it fell open—Romans 13. The words burned into his mind: "not in orgies and drunkenness, not in sexual immorality and debauchery, not in dissension and jealousy. Rather clothe yourselves with the Lord Jesus Christ, and do not think about how to gratify the desires of the sinful nature" (vv. 13-14). Instantly, the shadows of his heart fled before the streams of light. A book he once dismissed as a mere fable lacking in clarity and grace of expression altered the entire trajectory of his life and gave him what he had sought for so long. He had encountered *truth.*

Augustine gave his life to Christ. And for the next forty-four years, Augustine continued to "take up and read," becoming one of the most influential Christian thinkers and writers of history. But it all started in the garden, where he learned that the Scriptures were not just words to be interpreted; they were words that interpreted the *reader.*

Little wonder that J. I. Packer once wrote, "If I were the devil . . . I should broadcast doubts about the truths and relevance and good sense and straightforwardness of the Bible. . . . At all costs I should want to keep them from using their minds in a disciplined way to get the measure of its message."

FOUR

The Lost Tools of Learning

"It would be a pity if we overlooked the possibilities
of education as a means of acquiring wisdom . . .
and if we lost our respect for learning."

T. S. ELIOT

In our world, knowledge is on the decline, with wisdom on an even more rapid descent. What is taking its place is *information,* virtually unlimited amounts coupled with immediate access. The founders of Google, one of the leading Internet search engines, took their name from *googol* (the numeral 1 followed by 100 zeros), signifying how much information they initially hoped to catalog. So one can "Google" God and come up with millions of "hits"—but what does this deliver? How do we wade through such vast amounts of information? What is right, what is wrong, what is reputable, what is without merit?

Quentin Schultze writes that such forays often leave us with little more than "endless volleys of nonsense, folly and rumor masquerading as knowledge, wisdom, and even truth." At the least, it is information without coherence—there is no organizing whole. It is fragmented, disassembled and piecemeal. Even worse, there are no gatekeepers, no counselors and no guides. It is the Wild West without a sheriff, a darkened alley without police patrol.

The inadequacy of this cannot be overstated, particularly as this information is not simply at our demand but under our control. We live in a world where we can see only what we choose to see, hear only what we choose to hear and read only what we choose to read. Through technology, we have the ability to filter out everything but what we wish to be exposed to—creating what University of Chicago professor Cass Sunstein has called the "Daily Me," a self-created world in which we see only the sports highlights that concern our favorite team, read only the issues that address our interests and engage only the op-ed pieces with which we agree.

The highly lauded personalization of information protects us from exposure to anything that might challenge our thinking or make us uncomfortable. Unchecked, we begin to follow the sound of nothing more than the echo of our own voice. At the very least, knowledge becomes trivialized. So as laudable as Google's project may be, the most popular Google searches of 2005 included Janet Jackson, Xbox 360, Brad Pitt, Michael Jackson, *American Idol* and Angelina Jolie.

This is why education matters.

And having it matter is, of course, quite Christian. The very foundation of liberal arts education can be traced back to the monastic education developed during the Middle Ages. There was sacred learning through the Bible and secular learning through the seven liberal arts of the trivium (grammar, rhetoric and logic) and quadrivium (arithmetic, geometry, astronomy and music). The idea was that the whole of human learning could be gathered into these "arts."

But the sacred-secular divide was not pronounced. The liberal arts were aimed at something beyond themselves, as evidenced in the very words *trivium* and *quadrivium*—the "threefold way" and the "fourfold way"—referring the way to the wisdom contained in the Word of God. In other words, such learning was decisive for the development of a Christian mind, for all truth was God's truth. Learning, in and of itself, was sacred, for it was pursuing the very knowledge of God, and life in light of that knowledge. The idea was the simultaneous cultivation of character and knowledge—and that the two were, in fact, inseparable.

T. S. Eliot wrote of the tragedy of losing our respect for learning. If all truth is God's truth, then truth is to be celebrated wherever it is found—and to be pursued wherever it can be found. Inherent within the idea of learning is placing ourselves in situations and experiences that allow such learning to take place. Reading is certainly a part of this, but reading that is separate from dialogue and instruction, guidance and challenge, creates a rather narrow learning experience. There is much to learn from others and from the interaction others have had with the books we have read. In Proverbs, the Bible speaks of our interaction with others as being akin to iron sharpening iron, one person sharpening another (Proverbs 27:17). I may have read the works of Shakespeare, but to study under someone who has devoted his or her life to Shakespeare is well worth the investment and holds far more than reading alone ever could. Otherwise I may fall prey to narrow thinking, limited opinion and often shallow conclusions.

But there is more for the Christian. The Bible speaks clearly of the spiritual gift of teaching (Romans 12:7; 1 Corinthians 12:29; Ephesians 4:11). Spiritual gifts are given by the Holy Spirit because they are needed by the body of Christ. The gift of teaching implies that there are students. And it means we need to be students. It is not an option but an implicit command. We must be learners, and one of the primary ways we are to learn is through teachers—this is so important the Holy Spirit actually distributes the gift of teaching for this very purpose. Failing to take advantage of this entails refusing the work of the Holy Spirit in our life. We are not to be indiscriminate learners, for not all teachers are Spirit-gifted, much less Spirit-led, but learning itself is not an option.

This is a radically different perspective on learning than that which currently dominates our world. Our tendency is to embrace what Clifford Williams terms a "utilitarian" view of education. We think of something like college as a way to ensure our place in the larger culture. We take courses so that we can enhance our resumés and get better jobs. At best, we study computer science, chemistry and biology in order to improve communication, transportation and medical technologies. At worst, we use them as a means to an end—that end most often being financial gain.

"The point of an education, the culture declares, is to better oneself by gaining skills and knowledge that will be useful in the marketplace," Williams maintains. "Rarely is the idea of learning as a good in itself mentioned." Yet if the mind is a creation of God to be stewarded as much as any other part of our existence, education can and should be seen—in and of itself—as intrinsically good. As Williams concludes, "attending school is not just a means of preparing for a good life. It is a good life."

CHRISTIAN LITERACY

So what should we commit ourselves to learning? Are there certain things we are to "know"? The respected academic E. D. Hirsch, who burst onto the cultural scene in the late 1980s, captured the attention of the wider populace with a simple idea, followed by an ambitious project. His idea was the value of "cultural literacy," meaning the importance of having a core of background knowledge for functional literacy and effective national communication. His project? To catalog what that literacy would entail. His book *Cultural Literacy* became a bestseller. Hirsch has cataloged over six thousand names, phrases, dates and concepts that he considers "essential." The same year another academic, Allan Bloom, published the bestseller *The Closing of the American Mind.* Though Bloom lamented far more than the loss of cultural literacy, he joined with Hirsch in the call for a return to a common denominator within education. These men ignited a national debate about the nature of education and the meaning of literacy. Questions swirled around the form and content of such knowledge, and whether education can actually be reduced to such things. But the central thesis remained: *there are certain things we should know.*

They were right.

There is a body of knowledge that lends itself to cultural literacy—and even further, *Christian* literacy. This is why as a professor of theology I teach certain things and not others, and then (along with every other teacher) proclaim, "You will need to know this for the test." The understanding inherent within education is that there are certain facts that should be known, books that should be read, lives that should be studied, events that should be remembered, and ideas that should be understood.

So what are those things?

Biblical literacy. The church has felt the need to identify what should be known from the earliest days. Luke, along with Matthew, Mark and John, felt it critical to pull together the *central* teachings and life events of Jesus, with John acknowledging, "Jesus did many other things as well. If every one of them were written down, I suppose that even the whole world would not have room for the books that would be written" (John 21:25).

And reflecting the importance of a core knowledge beyond the Gospels, God gave us the rest of the Scriptures. God boiled the law down to ten commandments; we need to know what they are—along with Jesus' Sermon on the Mount, the seven letters to the seven churches, the wisdom of the Proverbs, the great theological treatise of Romans, the evangelistic thrust of John's Gospel and everything else within the canon.

So the starting point of our education (or our commitment to learning) is biblical literacy. In terms of overall literacy, this is arguably where the church has done its best, where the spiritual gift of teaching has been most recognized and where Christians have most devoted themselves as students. But we are always one generation away from biblical *illiteracy*. Learning the Bible is an ongoing challenge that lies in the vanguard of our commitment to education. We simply must become students of the Scriptures, sitting under teachers devoted to the Scriptures and forming a deep understanding of God's Word.

Historical literacy. Beyond biblical learning, there are certain events in history, specifically Christian history (which is often overlooked by Christians), that should be known. And not simply dates, names and places, but more importantly *significance*.

History, as has often been noted, is "his story"—meaning the story of God's activities in the world. It is common knowledge that to ignore history is to be condemned to repeat it. More to the point, to ignore history is to ignore our world, the people that have shaped it and the current of events that have brought us to where we are. It would be difficult to imagine a Christian mind operating without such knowledge.

The ultimate authority within the Christian faith is the triune God. The Trinity is revealed first and foremost in Scripture, but we also must drink deeply from its conveyance through our Christian heritage. History is certainly secondary to Scripture—it is informative, not normative—but it does *inform*. History is walking back through time, listening to its better minds. We sometimes imagine that the issues of our day did not exist before our day, but this is a grave mistake. The church has previously wrestled with most of our issues, and those "wrestlings" are well worth our time to explore, or we cut ourselves off from the accumulated wisdom and insight of the ages.

So what significant events should be known—at least in terms of Christian history? Historian Mark Noll has suggested the following twelve as seminal: the fall of Jerusalem (A.D. 70), the council of Nicaea (325), the council of Chalcedon (451), Benedict's Rule (530), the coronation of Charlemagne (800), the "great schism" between the Eastern and Western church (1054), the Diet of Worms (1521), the English Act of Supremacy (1534), the founding of the Jesuits (1540), the conversion of the Wesleys (1738), the French Revolution (1789), and the Edinburgh Missionary Conference (1910).

In decisive ways, these events, as well as many others, have shaped the church and the way it interacts with the world. Understanding the significance of such events is indispensable to interacting with the world in positive and productive ways. Failing to do so is akin to joining a conversation that is well under way without any sense of what has already been said.

Theological literacy. Beyond biblical and historical literacy is theological literacy. Theology is built from two Greek words: *theos* (God) and *logos* (word). Thus *theology* means "words about God," the great attempt to pull together what can be said about God and the things of God. The Bible is God's revelation; history walks us through how some of the better minds have wrestled with it; theology puts it all together and applies it to the great questions of life and to our spiritual formation. If the Bible tells us the "what," theology attempts to give the "so what."

In pulling this together, theology has traditionally organized itself in ten categories: (1) the existence, nature and attributes of God (theology proper); (2) revelation (the inspiration and authority of Scripture); (3) creation and providence; (4) humanity and human nature; (5) original and actual sin; (6) the person and work of Christ; (7) sin and grace; (8) the person and work of the Holy Spirit; (9) the church; and (10) the end times.

Each of these areas is critical to explore and understand. We say we believe in the God of the Bible—so what kind of God is God: personal or impersonal, caring or indifferent? We say we believe the Bible—in what way: as truth without mixture of error or as simply a relatively reliable guide? If we hold to the Bible's inspiration, do we mean "inspired" in the sense of Bach's Brandenburg Concertos or something more? We say we believe in creation and that humans are made in the image of God—but what does that mean? Where is the image located? When does life even begin? What gives it value?

These are theological questions. Before a mind can contend with culture, it must first ground itself in a sound and vibrant Christian theology. This is why theology was called the "queen" of the sciences throughout the medieval era. There was no other field of study, no other topic, which held greater worth.

GETTING AN EDUCATION

Of course, talking about education and actually getting it are two different things. Where do Christians go to learn theology or church history? In times past this took place in churches and the seminaries that serve them. Unfortunately, this is often no longer the case. So churches and seminaries must rise to the educational challenge.

Fortunately, many are.

Churches are increasingly taking a community college approach to their educational ministries. The church I belong to offers an institute for adults with a fresh slate of courses—from Christian theology to Bible 101 to church history to book studies—each quarter. Such learning opportunities are seen as a vital "third leg" to the learning stool, complementing weekend and midweek services and small group experiences.

Seminaries are beginning to think outside of the standard educational box. Many of the larger seminaries are offering branch campuses and extension centers in key population centers throughout the United States. Even more are using the Internet to offer distance learning programs. Others have produced CD-ROMs that include audio lectures and lecture outlines, study guides and study questions, and bibliographies for further reading. Companion websites provide further resources and allow significant interaction among students, and between students and instructors.

But we are not strictly dependent on traditional institutions for the development of our minds. Audio journals, mentoring programs, book discussion groups, community colleges, online libraries and study programs abound.

The issue is taking advantage of them.[†]

EDUCATION AND EDUCATORS

As you might imagine, the importance of education highlights the importance of educators—not simply within the life of the church or the seminary but in academia in general. Christians committed to a life of learning must lift high the calling to be an educator, for

---

[†]An introductory list of resources for continued education is provided in appendix two, "Resources for Learning."

it is a call in desperate need of being answered.

Recently, a Brooklyn College professor dropped his bid to become chairman of the department of sociology due to outrage over his description of religious people as "moral retards." In an essay he published in an online journal, he argued that religious people are incapable of moral action, and that "self-righteousness, paranoia, and hatred" characterize Christians in particular. An apparently earlier version of the online essay added, "Christians claim that theirs is a faith based on love, but they'll just as soon kill you." He even suggests that Christians have a greater proclivity toward child molestation.

Unfortunately, such outrageous campus rhetoric is not unusual. Obviously the relationship between Christians and the academy is a challenging one. But it has not always been that way, and it can be changed. Thus there is a desperate need for Christians to not only obtain an education but also pursue a scholarly vocation within the academy—for the express purpose of making a mark for God in that arena, serving and equipping the next generation of learners.

The aforementioned Brooklyn College, which has more than fifteen thousand students, recently observed its seventy-fifth anniversary. It was named one of the top ten best values among undergraduate institutions in the country by the *Princeton Review.* But Brooklyn College is more than that. Like every other institution devoted to higher education, it is a mission field filled with students who, according to many seasoned observers, are in their best season for responding to Christ. And as Daniel Tauber, president-elect of Brooklyn College's student government lamented, "I would like to see professors in high positions who don't believe religious people are moral retards."

In *The Outrageous Idea of Christian Scholarship,* historian George Marsden observes that the "contemporary university culture is hollow at its core." Or as a Harvard Law School professor once expressed, many professors have become like "priests who have lost their faith, and kept their jobs." There is a highly significant need, argues Marsden, for explicit discussion of the relationship between religious faith and learning. But this can only be pursued if Christians answer God's call to the university, and from that position relate their belief in God—a Christian worldview—to all thinking.

Sadly, Marsden notes that even Christians scholars have not reflected much on the relationship of their faith to their intellectual life. Imagine if they did—becoming models for thousands more to follow, who then used their positions to encourage generations of learners in Christ.

FIVE

Sacred Thinking

"We live forward, but we can only think backward."

SØREN KIERKEGAARD

*I*n his fourteenth encyclical, *Fides et Ratio* (Faith and Reason), Pope John Paul II expressed dismay that philosophers no longer wrestle with the big questions of life, the questions that most define who we are: What does it all mean? Does life have a purpose? Is death the end? Is there a God? If it is increasingly rare among philosophers, we can only imagine the degree of scarcity among the rest of us.

To *reflect* means to give thought to something to such a degree that it brings some kind of realization—an *aha* moment. It takes an idea and lives with it until it is burned deep within. It takes a question and, like Jacob wrestling with the angel, does not let it go until some form of answer emerges. Christian reflection takes what is read, taught, suggested and announced, and brings it into confrontation with a biblical worldview. It is thinking Christianly.

It is significant that the Latin word *schola,* from which we get our words *scholar* and *scholarship,* means "free time," joining the importance of fallow time given over to reflection for true intellectual development. In order to nurture the life of the mind, we must protect the time it takes to practice it. Most think this means time devoted to study; in truth, it means the time to study coupled with the time needed to *reflect* on what we have studied. Otherwise we will be engaging the worst of Malcolm Gladwell's famed "blink"— how we tend to make immediate assessments about things— which can lead to responding without thinking on things that *need* to be thought about.

Henri Nouwen insightfully wonders if the fact that so many people ask support, advice and counsel from so many other people is not, in large part, due to their having lost contact with the practice of such reflection. Sometimes one feels, writes Nouwen, "as if one half of the world is asking advice of the other half while both sides are sitting in the same darkness."

The dynamics of reflection are not difficult to process. Christian reflection involves times of silence and solitude, prayer, and immersion into the Scriptures. On the front end, we take conversations and counsel, reading and experience with us. The authority over all reflection is, of course, holy Scripture, but reflection should not be reduced to Bible study. The complexity of the world and our lives within it depend on the Bible but demand the application of the Bible that only reflection can bring.

As I often challenge my students, the Bible gives us all we *must* know, but not all that there *is* to know. Bringing Scripture to bear on something such as bioethics involves taking the Bible's foundational teaching on creation and what it means to be human, along with the important scriptural teachings on the sanctity of human life, and then reflecting on the implications of such truths in terms of the technological advancements and opportunities of our day. To fall back and declare "The Bible doesn't say anything about bioethics" is simply not true. Of course it does. But its application takes a willing and educated mind bent on reflection. Great Christian thinkers are often those who have simply taken the time to do it.

Reflection does more, though, than bring insight. It brings a sensitivity, an awareness of things. It provides penetrating insight, an intuitive assessment of the world that cannot come any other way. I recall listening to a lecture at Oxford by the great mystery writer P. D. James on the interplay between Christian theology and her mysteries. She said she was often asked how she could write about murder as a Christian. Her answer was that she was writing about the human condition, including sin, and murder brought that condition into the clearest of lights. She also liked separating fact from fiction. She then added that the world needs such clear thinking, rooted in reflection, "For there is much in our world that is clever," she said, "yet is not true." This is what reflection brings to the surface—separating fact from fiction, the merely clever from the true.

Consider the media, perhaps the most important challenge facing Christian reflection. At its most base, the media tell us both what to think about and then how to think about it. Sociologist Christian Smith writes that we may talk about "the culture," "the media," "television" and "Hollywood," but if we think systemically, these are euphemisms for a worldview that constitutes the human self in a very particular way: as an autonomous, rational, self-seeking, cost-benefit calculating consumer. This constitutes a moral order with particular assumptions, narratives, commitments, beliefs, values and goals.

Malcolm Muggeridge tells of taking Mother Teresa into a New York television studio to appear on one of the morning shows. It was the first time that Mother Teresa had been in an American television studio, and as a result she was completely unprepared for the constant interruptions for commercials.

On that particular morning, Muggeridge observed that all of the commercials dealt with food that was being advertised as non-fattening and low in calories. Mother Teresa took it in with a sense of unbelief. Her own work was in trying to nourish the starving, to put some flesh on human skeletons. Suddenly, without even thinking, she said out loud, "I see that Christ is needed in television studios."

A total silence fell on the studio and everyone there. Muggeridge said that in the midst of the media fantasy, reality had suddenly intruded.

But it took someone being still and reflecting on what reality entailed. Because of the influences of the media on our world—and our minds—the dynamics of reflection on cultural discourse (which is generally carried out through the media) is decisive. Few of us would have thought twice about the commercial content, much less the messages they were sending, that was so evident to Mother Teresa. But that is where a Christian mind, practiced in reflection, comes into play—and is most needed. For as T. S. Eliot once quipped, "Paganism holds all the most valuable advertising space."

We cannot simply afford to reflect on what culture tells us to know; we also must reflect on what it tells us to *feel.* By getting someone to feel a certain way, you can lead them to a certain belief *through* those feelings. In an ABC news story on the death of Princess Diana, Andrew Morton said that Diana's death was "one of the most awful tragedies of the late 20th century, if not the greatest. . . . In her death something inside us had died. . . . People are grieving for lost hopes, lost dreams, lost ambitions."

That is a very emotional assessment. The continual scenes of grief and crying led us to feel that this was a loss of historic proportions. Yet this simply wasn't the case. Nothing against Diana, much less those who grieved her passing, but not only was her death far from the greatest tragedy that has occurred to the world over the previous fifty years—eclipsing such things as the Vietnam War, Chernobyl, Tiananmen Square or the explosion of the space shuttle *Challenger*—but even when compared to the loss of other figures, such as Mother Teresa who died the same week, she lived a life of very little significance. As has been said on more than one occasion, she was mostly famous for being famous. Yet her death greatly overshadowed Mother Teresa's because we were led to *feel* that way by the media, so much so that the talk was not that Mother Teresa would be made a saint but that Princess Diana would.

There are many other ways that the media leads us in our feelings. One of the most powerful is through repetition—putting certain alternate choices or lifestyles before us over and over again. Eventually we become so desensitized to reality and the truth that we accept those choices and lifestyles as normal. If the repetitive behavior is exhibited through a character that is particularly likable, the influence is all the more great.

Sexual behavior is a prime example. MTV is often criticized for the incessant sleaze of steamy programming aimed at young people. The critics are not being unreasonable. During a single week in March 2004 the Parents Television Council (PTC) recorded 3,056 flashes of nudity or sexual situations and 2,881 verbal references to sex on MTV. Beyond sexual content, the PTC said it recorded 3,127 instances of "bleeped" profane dialogue and another 1,518 other instances of unedited rough language.

But television as a whole is becoming increasingly sexual. According to a study of the 2004-2005 TV season by the Kaiser Family Foundation, the number of sexual scenes has nearly doubled over an earlier study in 1998. Now seven out of every ten shows have sexual content, averaging five sex scenes per hour.

If the portrayals of premarital sex in the media outnumber sex within marriage—which study after study demonstrates is clearly the case—then premarital sex becomes normal in our thinking. If characters are portrayed as having intercourse after they have just met—and the amount of such portrayals doubled between 1998 and 2004—then that will increasingly be seen as mainstream behavior. As George Lucas, one of the most successful filmmakers in Hollywood history, once said, "For better or worse . . . films and television tell us the way we conduct our lives, what is right and wrong."

I once read a speech given by film director Oliver Stone at American University. Stone is well known for such films as *Natural Born Killers, Platoon* and *JFK.* In responding to the distortions and factual errors in his films, particularly *JFK* (presented as a fauxdocumentary on the Kennedy assassination), Stone said that films should not be the end-all for what is true, saying that people "have a responsibility to read a book." Nobody, he said, "is going to sit through a three-hour movie and say, 'That's that.'"

He is wrong. That is exactly what people do—and that is precisely what must end. In his famed reminder to H. G. Wells, G. K. Chesterton quipped that the object of opening the mind, as of opening the mouth, is to shut it again on something solid. It has been said that the electronic world has meant a "speeded-up mind," which is precisely what we cannot afford. As Søren Kierkegaard once counseled, "We live forward, but we can only think backward."

AN INTEGRATED WORLDVIEW

To engage in such reflection, we must have an integrated sense of things, as opposed to succumbing to a kind of compartmentalization that fails to address the entirety of life. A compartmentalized mind is one that separates aspects of life into distinct categories—job, family, HBO, a quiet time, the business section of the newspaper and AOL—*all without integration.* Our thinking about one area never informs our thinking about another.

Thus a person can be a Christian but not reflect about science or technology in light of faith. Or even worse, never even have the *thought* come to mind of reflecting about science or technology in light of faith. So issues related to bioethics are seldom met with a Christian mind that has reflected on the nature of humanity and the sanctity of human life in the light of Scripture. Instead, we simply let CNN tell us what various scientific and technological breakthroughs will mean for the quality of our life; we marvel at progress; and then we ponder whether we will be able to afford the procedure. The world of science becomes distinct from the world of faith. To his credit, this is the critique inherent in Michael Crichton's novel and subsequent film *Jurassic Park.* "You were so busy pursuing what you could do," says Ian Malcolm, the scientist portrayed by Jeff Goldblum, to the founder of the park, "that you never stopped to ask yourself if you should do it."

Even when it comes to scholarship, the question is not simply over facts but over reflective interpretation of those facts. George

Marsden gives the example of the Battle of Little Bighorn. Two historians might be able to agree perfectly well on the details—where and when it took place, how many people were killed on both sides, and (perhaps) who fired the first shot. Nonetheless, one scholar might see the battle as Custer's heroic last stand in a fight to bring peace to the American West; another might see it as a triumph in the Native American fight to resist barbaric invaders. "While at one level such differences might look like mere partisanship," Marsden writes, "at a deeper level they have to do with large-scale beliefs about what the world is, or should be, like." Mark Noll casts the vision for the comprehensive nature of this kind of thinking by speaking of the "life of the mind":

> By an evangelical "life of the mind" I mean . . . the effort to think like a Christian—to think within a specifically Christian framework—across the whole spectrum of modern learning, including economics and political science, literary criticism and imaginative writing, historical inquiry and philosophical studies, linguistics and the history of science, social theory and the arts.

This is the essence of the idea of a Christian worldview.** The term *worldview,* from the German *Weltanschauung* (literally, "world perception"), suggests more than a set of ideas by which you judge

---

** On pp. 103-4 of the "Book Lists" appendix, I offer a beginning list of books designed to serve a Christian worldview.

other ideas. It is, as Gene Edward Veith has written, "a way to engage constructively the whole range of human expression from a Christian perspective." Or as Jonathan Edwards, arguably the greatest intellect America has ever produced, once contended, the basic goal of any mind is to work toward "the consistency and agreement of our ideas with the ideas of God."

So the Christian mind gives radically different answers to what James Sire reasonably puts forward as the seven basic questions for any worldview: What is ultimate reality? What is the nature of the world around us? What does it mean to be human? What happens when I die? On what basis are we able to know anything at all? How do we determine right or wrong? What is the meaning of history? Or from a more theological point of view, consider the worldview questions posed by Charles Colson and Nancy Pearcey: Where did we come from and who are we? What has gone wrong with the world? What can we do to fix it? How now shall we live?

Consider the Christian response to the first and most foundational of these questions—where did we come from? There are a limited number of answers at our disposal: (1) we came about by chance (the naturalist contention), (2) we don't really exist (the Hindu response), or (3) we were spoke into existence by God. Even when people, such as the discoverer of DNA, Francis Crick, suggest that we were seeded here by another race of beings from another planet, they would then have to account for the existence of these other beings. So for the Christian, the answer to "Where did we come from, and who are we?" gives a foundation for thinking that no other answer gives. Because we were created, each person has value, and there is meaning and purpose to every life. There is Someone above and outside of our existence who stands over us as our authority.

Because of this answer, Martin Luther King Jr. could write the immortal words found in his letter from the Birmingham jail:

> There are two types of law: just and unjust. . . . A just law is a man-made code that squares with the moral law or the law of God. An unjust law is a code that is out of harmony with the moral law. . . . Any law that uplifts human personality is just. Any law that degrades human personality is unjust. All segregation statutes are unjust because segregation distorts the soul and damages the personality.

King's argument was based on the dignity and worth bestowed by God on all humans, regardless of what other humans might have to say. He laid claim to a law above human law. No other worldview would have given King the basis for such a claim. And from such a worldview, the world was changed.

But worldviews such as King's are increasingly rare.

THE DANGER OF AN UNREFLECTIVE LIFE

A new graduate from Baylor University confessed to one of her professors that her college curriculum did not require her life to be formed by serious thinking *or* living. While she assimilated great reams of *information* during her four years in the university, she admitted that she did almost no *thinking:* no tough-minded engagement with life-shaping books and ideas. Her honors degree had never required her to encounter the overarching moral and religious questions or to undertake any serious reevaluation of her life. She admitted the truthfulness of Walker Percy's aphorism that "you can make all A's and still flunk life."

And flunking life in this way can take on nightmarish scenarios.

Kay Haugaard, a professor in Southern California, made this chilling report in *The Chronicle of Higher Education.*

Her twenty students were discussing Shirley Jackson's short story "The Lottery," found in numerous literary anthologies designed for students. Set in a small town in rural America, the townsfolk gather for a seemingly innocent ritual deemed critical for the well-being of the crops and the community, of which the center of attention is a lottery. Mothers and fathers, sons and daughters, come forward to draw pieces of paper. There is great anxiety as they draw their paper; deep relief when they find it blank. Suddenly, the story reveals the frightening truth that the draw is for a human sacrifice. In the end, a woman draws the slip of paper marked by a black spot. Stones are gathered; she is circled—and killed.

Even her small son had pebbles in his hand.

When the *New Yorker* first published the essay in 1948, it was met by a storm of outrage. The story's moral—the danger of "going along" in blind social conformity—was repugnant to the generation that had stood up to Hitler.

Times change.

On the warm California night that brought chills to Haugaard, her class registered no moral response at all.

"The end was neat!" one woman offered.

"If it's a part of a person's culture, . . . and if it has worked for them, [it's okay]," another suggested.

"At this point I gave up," wrote Haugaard. "No one in the whole class of twenty ostensibly intelligent individuals would go out on a limb and take a stand [even] against human sacrifice."

SIX

A Rule for the Mind

*"As iron rusts when not used,
and water gets foul from standing or turns to ice when exposed
to cold, so the intellect degenerates without exercise."*

LEONARDO DA VINCI

I recently downloaded a training schedule for completing a triathlon. It involved a certain number of workouts on a certain number of days, with increasing intensity and duration as the event drew near. It called for cross-training in swimming, biking and running, which make up a triathlon. Along with the workouts, it built in days of rest and suggested dietary regimens.

If I followed the plan, I was assured of being ready for the competition. *But I had to follow the plan.* I had to subscribe to a set of practices that would enable me to achieve what I desired.

This makes perfect sense to us for physical achievement. It even makes sense in plotting our career goals and financial goals.

It is less common to think of it in terms of our spiritual lives, much less how our relationship with Christ calls us to develop our minds.

But this is the nature of an ancient spiritual practice called a "rule," which can be traced back to the founding of Benedictine monasticism. Penned at the beginning of the sixth century, Benedict wished to write a rule that would help guide monks to holiness. By "rule," he intended a guide for optimal spiritual formation. Thomas Moore writes that "every thoughtful person, no matter what his or her lifestyle may be, has a rule," meaning a pattern or model for living.

Few of us live lives—or more to the point, *have* lives—that lend themselves to reading, learning and reflection. We work in the home, office or factory forty to fifty hours a week, or if still in school, carry a heavy course load that allows little discretionary time. We have clothes to wash, checkbooks to balance, e-mails to read, soccer games to attend. The world is very real, and we live in it as real people. What we *should* do and what we *can* do often feel like radically different things, and the discouragement and defeat that comes with the chasm between them is ever present.

But that's not all. Most of us work in places where the ultimate virtue is "success" and the god on the throne is money. The vast majority of our colleagues do not share our relationship with Christ. While this holds great promise for personal evangelism, it holds equal peril in regard to our minds. We are immersed in a context that wars against taking captive every thought for Christ. Our dilemma is that we do not have the time to develop our minds, and where we are forced to spend our time tears apart what little of a Christian mind we have.

We need to recapture a sense that the development of our minds is a spiritual discipline. We must do it intentionally, and even counterculturally. Unfortunately, many Christians do not see how study and reflection can be spiritual disciplines. Yet Dallas Willard writes that a spiritual discipline is *any* activity "undertaken to bring us into more effective cooperation with Christ and His Kingdom."

To the Romans the apostle Paul said, "This is your spiritual act of worship. Do not conform any longer to the pattern of this world, but be transformed by the renewing of your mind" (Romans 12:1-2). And in speaking of the transformation *itself,* the tense of the Greek verb is the present imperative; thus Paul is literally saying "keep on" being transformed through the *ongoing* renewal of your mind.

Our very transformation as Christians is dependent on whether our minds are engaged in an ongoing process of renewal in light of Christ. Our minds are deeply spiritual, and so developing our minds must be a spiritual discipline. Or as Os Guinness has written, our passion is not for academic respectability but for faithfulness to the commands of Jesus: "thinking Christianly is first and foremost a matter of love—of minds in love with God and the truth of his world."

Rules are not merely lofty ambitions but gritty realities that must be pursued in the midst of daily decisions. If we do not impose a will or intent on our lives, they will be buffeted by every circumstance, every "urgency," every demand that comes our way. And we will seldom if ever sit down and read a book, take time to reflect or engage in learning experiences. We must lay claim to our life before other things lay claim to it for us.

To develop and then maintain a Christian mind, we need a *real* rule. Something that will take the scattered, frantic activities of life and carve out space and time needed to honor God with the full development of our intellect. The key is *discipline.* This is what a rule is—an organized set of practices we follow in order to tend to things that we would not tend to otherwise.

Every rule, in this sense, will be different. And rules will also change depending on our season of life (a young mother's rule will be vastly different than the woman's enjoying her grandchildren) and whether or not it is an intellectual rule, a devotional rule, a physical rule, and so on. But what is constant for us all is the need to drive stakes in the ground and declare "This I will do" or "This I will maintain" as a matter of ordering our life.

This is the nature of a rule—a set of disciplines, decisions and impositions we make on our life in order to prevent the tyranny of the urgent from stealing time away. With a rule, we achieve what we most want. If we don't, then time will escape us. It will be taken up by the mundane, by what screams the loudest, by what tempts us most, and we will not have the time to develop our minds the way God has called us to develop them.

So what should our rule look like?

DEVELOPING A RULE FOR READING

Borrowing a phrase from Thomas Jefferson, Susan Wise Bauer rightly maintains that any literate man or woman can develop a rule for reading. "All you need are a shelf full of books . . . and a few 'chasms of time not otherwise appropriated.' " With the scent of a savvy, real-world reader, Bauer gives the following suggestions: morning is better than evening (why fight the fatigue?); start short (as with physical exercise, work your way into shape, starting with no more than thirty minutes a day); don't schedule yourself for reading every day of the week (aim for four days, giving yourself some days off for the inevitable interruptions of life); never check your e-mail right before you start reading (if you have e-mail, you know how it distracts the mind and commands your time); guard your reading time (set it, keep it, protect it); and take the first step *now*.

I would add three more to her list (beyond those offered in the earlier chapter on reading): Do not attempt to read a book, particularly a significant one, in the context of chaos. Blaring music, kids running amuck and getting up to answer the phone—such distractions are insurmountable. To guard your reading, it is not enough to put time itself aside; you must protect its quality.

Second, do not become discouraged if you read slowly, resulting in only a few books a year. The more you read, the faster you will read. The same is true with comprehension. Your mind is like your body; you should not expect to run a four-minute mile the first day or complete a marathon after two weeks in the gym. Speed and increased abilities in reading comprehension come with time. And they *will* come.

Finally, reading is served by knowing how individual books should be read. Not every book qualifies for a cover-to-cover journey. Long ago, Francis Bacon gave this wise counsel: "Some books are to be tasted, others to be swallowed, and some few to be chewed and digested." Read each book to the degree that it deserves, and no more. A classic text that will help in this area is Mortimer Adler's *How to Read a Book*.

Most people would be amazed at what can be accomplished with such practices. Will Durant, winner of the Pulitzer Prize and author of the famed eleven-volume *The Story of Civilization,* once listed "the one hundred 'best' books for an education." As if he anticipated the reaction to such a program, he writes, "Can you spare one hour a day? . . . Let me have seven hours a week, and I will make a scholar and a philosopher out of you; in four years you shall be as well educated as any new-fledged Doctor of Philosophy in the land."

DEVELOPING A RULE FOR LEARNING

A rule for learning will look for ways to put learning into our lives that is regular and purposeful. The easiest of steps might be a class each semester through a church or community college. Take advantage of a nearby seminary or Internet-based seminary programs. A regularly scheduled class provides a rule of its own in terms of time and frequency, forcing other time demands to bend.

There are increasing opportunities to combine vacations with learning experiences, such as through a cruise or summer continuing education at a college or university. An excellent example is the biannual Oxbridge event sponsored by the C. S. Lewis Foundation, which provides one week in Oxford and a second week in Cambridge.

Such events can be mapped out far in advance and scheduled around the realities and complexities of your life. But an even simpler rule is to take advantage of the vast array of tapes, CDs and downloadable MP3 files. Through such resources we can turn workouts at the gym and rush-hour traffic into a classroom for our minds. This past year I have used such times to take college-level courses in Einstein's physics as well as medieval history. The simple rule I established uses my daily driving times—the commute to the office, picking my kids up from school, driving to an event—for learning. My wife routinely goes through books of the Bible this way, having purchased the entire Bible on CD.

DEVELOPING A RULE FOR REFLECTION

In his catalog of wisdom and sayings from the desert fathers of the fourth century, Thomas Merton tells of a certain brother who asked Abbot Moses of Scete for a good word. The elder said to him, "Go, sit in your cell, and your cell will teach you everything." The power of silence and solitude has been recognized throughout the history of spiritual formation, and both lie at the heart of developing a rule for reflection. It is important to remember the difference between spiritual quietness and the mere absence of sound that creates silence. "Silence is the absence of sound and quiet the stilling of sound," writes Frederick Buechner. "Quiet chooses to be silent. It holds its breath to listen."

The Rule of St. Benedict speaks of *cultivating* silence in our lives, with an entire chapter devoted to its pursuit. The point is to create times and places in order to *think*. We are physical creatures, living in space and time. As a result, space and time affect us in ways we seldom imagine and offer us either depth or superficiality in our thinking. Most of us are familiar with the practice of a daily quiet time in order to pray, read and reflect on the Bible, and perhaps journal a bit. But we must also have regular quiet times for the purpose of wrestling with an issue, thinking through a matter and attempting to gain an insight.

In my own life, I take a monthly retreat for this very purpose. The mountains of the Blue Ridge are a short drive from my home, so once a month I drive to a little bed and breakfast for an overnight stay. I leave on a Thursday afternoon, and as I drive toward the clean air and clear skies, I feel my mind beginning to expand

and go deep in ways that it simply could not have in the midst of the busyness of my normal world.

As soon as I arrive, I take a hike around a quiet lake. I pray. I think. Returning to my room, I read and reflect, journal and pray. I gaze over a seventy-mile vista. It is nothing less than the richest possible time for "reasoning together" with God that I cannot experience any other way.

Not everyone has the ability to travel to the mountains once a month, but the practice of retreat for the purpose of prayerful reflection *itself* is open to all. A solitary moment before dawn, a walk in a nearby park, a bench in a quiet garden. We can all *withdraw*. Doing so allows us to return with a fullness of spirit and a depth of thought that approaches the world with a clarity and keenness offsetting the emptiness of the world around us.

THE CHOICE BEHIND YOUR RULE

Again, we come to choices. We will drive in the car—will it be used for learning or mindless music and some inane banter between disc jockeys? We will take vacations—will we incorporate learning or simply shop and eat? We have seven evenings every week—will we take even an hour or two of those nights to read? A rule for learning is a matter of choice. The opportunities themselves are endless.

SEVEN

Thinking Out Loud

"One word of truth outweighs the world."

ALEKSANDR SOLZHENITSYN

Catholic scholar George Weigel writes that in June 1959 the commission preparing the agenda for the Second Vatican Council asked all the Catholic bishops of the world what they would like to talk about. A forty-year-old auxiliary bishop of Krakow named Karol Wojtyla—the future Pope John Paul II—sent a single, sharp question: What in the world has happened? How did the twentieth century, which had begun with such high expectations for the human future, produce within a handful of decades two world wars, three totalitarian systems, Auschwitz, the Gulag, mountains of corpses, oceans of blood, the greatest persecutions in Christian history, and a Cold War that threatened the future of the planet? *What happened?* What happened, Karol Wojtyla suggested, was that the great project of Western humanism had gone off the rails.

As John Paul's biographer, Weigel summarizes the thinking of the late pontiff: "Ideas have consequences, and bad ideas can have lethal consequences."

Our purpose in developing our minds is our love for God. Our mission, however, is to contend with the darkness for the sake of the light. We do not exercise our intellects merely to explore ideas and arguments. Those who study the history of Christianity as merely an *intellectual* history miss the point. As Robert Louis Wilken noted, "The study of . . . Christian thought has been too preoccupied with ideas. . . . Its mission . . . [is] to win the hearts and minds of men and women and to change their lives."

This is a clarion call for the Christian mind to engage in apologetics, which is arguably one of its most needed functions. From the Greek word *apologia,* which means to defend something, apologetics is giving a defense of the faith, reasons to believe, answers to the questions of the day. Through apologetics the mind supports the task of evangelism, clearing away barriers and objections so that faith may be examined at face value.

Historically, Christian apologetics has leaned toward providing rational evidence for the faith, but there is a growing need for something even more basic, which is a clear explanation of faith. In the world today, the deepest question regarding the Christian faith is "So what?" This is at the heart of both thinking Christianly and communicating Christianity to others. As Thomas Oden has observed, the fact of the resurrection may be maintained in the church, but there is often little interest or communication regarding the *significance* of the resurrection. Jesus was raised from the dead. *So what?* The Bible is true. *So what?* You can have a personal relationship with God. *So what?*

This is what the *Christian* mind must understand in order to challenge the *world's* mind to consider. If we cannot rise to this task, we will have lost our place in the most critical of conversations—indeed, the only conversation that matters.

The mission of the church is paramount, and what propels the mission forward is an awakened mind, a mind ablaze with God and the things of God. This is the heart of the cultural commission within the Great Commission. The Great Commission calls us to reach out to every person with the gospel of Jesus Christ; the cultural commission calls us to lay hold of every nook and cranny of our world for the kingdom of God. They are not separate endeavors—they are the two edges of the single sword we are to wield. Though frighteningly few Christians embrace the true dynamic and practice of the Great Commission, even fewer take hold of the cultural commission inherent within it. Too often we retreat into our Christian subculture, with its self-concerned books and magazines and radio stations and bumper stickers, sticking our heads in the sand oblivious to the world around us.

Henri Nouwen writes of a priest who told him that he cancelled his subscription to the *New York Times* because he felt that the endless stories about war, crime, power games and political manipulation only disturbed his mind and heart, and prevented him from meditation and prayer. "That is a sad story," writes Nouwen. "A real spiritual life does exactly the opposite: it makes us so alert and aware of the world around us, that all that is and happens becomes part of our contemplation and meditation and invites us to a free and fearless response."

This is the difference between a Christian who is *intelligent* and a Christian who has an *intellect*. No one, argues Richard Hofstadter, questions the value of intelligence, that excellence of mind employed with narrow, immediate, predictable ranges that are undeniably practical. Intellect, on the other hand, is the critical, creative and contemplative side of things.

It is also the activist side of things.

For our minds to break free and loom large on the world's stage, we must recapture the lost art of thinking itself. Having a Christian mind means to think—and to think widely and broadly. This goes beyond the practice of reflection, important as this practice is, for reflection is more of a discipline or skill to be embraced. But now we are talking about application—prayerfully setting the mind to the task at hand. Nouwen's friend purposefully avoided the *New York Times*. Nouwen's reminder should not be lost: the point is to purposefully engage the *New York Times*.

This brings us to the heart of the mind applied. It is not simply *thinking* Christianly, for to know is to *do*. Our goal is to think in order to know how to live. So what does it mean for Christ to lay claim to medicine? To law? To politics? To the economy? To a child in the womb? To sexuality? Consider the words of the prophet Micah:

> And what does the LORD require of you?
> To act justly and to love mercy
> and to walk humbly with your God. (Micah 6:8)

It is not enough to simply understand the nature of justice and love from within a Christian perspective. "We must go on," writes Dennis Hollinger, "to think about the strategies of justice and love in issues like poverty, race relations, abortion and political life."

This is the vanguard of Christian thinking—knowing how to live and then working to make the kingdom of God a reality for others to be able to live as well.

THE RESPONSIBILITY OF KNOWLEDGE

As important as a Christian mind is and the cultural commission inherent within it to engage the world accordingly, such pursuits are merely manifestations that flow from the ultimate goal of honoring God through a life lived in obedience to God. It is not simply knowing the truth, but living under it with a free and open heart in worship of the God of truth. This is the heart of wisdom, which is what every mind—and life—is to pursue.

Wisdom is not the same as common sense, at least as it is portrayed in the Bible, nor is it knowledge for knowledge's sake. Wisdom is the understanding of what God would have us do and then doing it, what God would have us think and then thinking it, what God would have us say and then saying it.

Throughout the Bible the wise person is the one who does the will of the Lord; the foolish person is the one who rebels. A believer's wisdom is found first in the acknowledgment of true wisdom and then in *obedience*. This is decisive, for there is a great breakdown between belief and behavior, knowing and doing. The heart of wisdom is their union, as is the heart of true knowledge.

So the greatest application of the mind is not cerebral—it is deeply personal. Its ultimate goal lies in what has been termed the *responsibility* of knowledge. "Sin," writes Os Guinness, "is a deliberate violation of the responsibility of knowledge." For to separate knowing from doing, belief from behavior, is the very nature of sin.

In his book *Intellectuals,* British historian Paul Johnson chronicles the life and thought of such great minds as Jean Jacques Rousseau, Karl Marx, Bertrand Russell and Jean Paul Sartre. He discovered that most of their arguments and philosophies were not based on noble convictions but on the choices they had made in their own lives.

For example, the eighteenth-century French philosopher Jean Jacques Rousseau had five children out of wedlock, and he abandoned them all. Then he maintained, supposedly out of his reasoning, intellect and common sense, that children do not need parents to give them discipline or guidance, and that the state should be responsible for raising them—an idea that is still shaping some educational and child-rearing theories to this day. His conclusions were not based on true reason but on his desire to justify the moral choices he had already made.

So the responsibility of knowledge comes down to nothing less than the lordship of Christ.

YOUR MIND FOR GOD

As I write these closing words, I'm sitting in the Eagle and Child pub in Oxford, England, the pub where (as the plaque on the wall reads):

> C. S. Lewis, his brother, W. H. Lewis, J. R. R. Tolkien, Charles Williams and other friends met every Tuesday morning, between the years 1939-1962 in the back room of this their favorite pub. These men, popularly known as the "Inklings," met here to drink beer and to discuss, among other things, the books they were writing.

I confess to loving English pubs, and particularly this one. The dark interior, the earthy atmosphere, the informal and congenial banter, and most of all the aura of the Inklings and their conversations that still seem to reverberate through the air. While I sit at my favorite little table, just to the side of the fireplace in the "rabbit room" (as it is now called) where the Inklings met, a stream of tourists enter, gaze at the pictures and memorabilia on the wall, and take their pictures. There is a sense of "this is where it happened" written on their faces.

But what, exactly, happened? What is it about Lewis and his friends that creates such a pilgrimage? What has made Lewis in particular the unofficial patron saint of so many Christians around the world?

Certainly not his life, as it was with a Mother Teresa. It has often been suggested that, due to his pipe-smoking, ale-drinking, free-speaking ways, he could not even be hired by the evangelical college that stewards his personal letters.

Unlike Billy Graham, Lewis didn't fill stadiums with his oratorical skills. (The only extant recording of which I'm aware is a snippet of him reading from his book *The Four Loves*.) Even the re-enactment of his famed sermon *The Weight of Glory,* which I heard given by the actor Joss Ackland (who played Lewis in the original BBC version of *Shadowlands*), was difficult listening.

We could argue that his imagination is what grips us—the fantasies of Narnia, the creativity of Screwtape—and that is certainly a part. But still, such things do not explain the esteem, even the reverence, in which C. S. Lewis is held. Even the fact that most Americans are closet Anglophiles doesn't quite complete the picture.

So what was it about Lewis?

It was his *mind.*

Lewis is a hero because he was a Christian intellect who stepped forward to engage the world. His Oxford education, his years teaching at Magdalen College (and then later at Cambridge), his abilities to speak of Chaucer and psychoanalysis, Beowulf and humanism, met a need in our spiritual lives that a thousand books on spiritual formation did not address. He was the twentieth century's most accomplished apologist for the Christian faith.

Who will be the C. S. Lewis of our day? As with figures like Mother Teresa and Billy Graham, there will not be a direct replacement—but the ministry of a Lewis is ever before us, for it is nothing less than a mind for God. One that is willing to think out loud.

But that will not be particularly welcome.

Actress Jada Pinkett Smith was honored as the "Artist of the Year" by the Harvard Foundation for Intercultural and Race Relations at the foundation's twentieth annual Cultural Rhythms show. In a speech many students considered inspirational and motivating, Pinkett Smith gave a warm, teary thank you and then shared life lessons with the audience. "Don't let anybody define who you are," she said. "Don't let them put you in a box." She told them about her childhood with teenage parents, both addicted to heroin, but triumphantly proclaimed, "I can stand here on this stage and say that I've proven them all wrong."

She then addressed issues regarding the roles of men and women today, specifically encouraging women to fight against the idea that choosing a career means having to choose against marriage and family. "Women, you can have . . . a loving man, devoted husband, loving children, . . . [and a] career. . . . All you have to do is want it." Pinkett Smith has been married to actor Will Smith since 1997 and is the mother of two children.

Though the Cultural Rhythms show is designed to feature culturally unique forms of artistic expression, along the lines of varying forms of music, the Bisexual, Gay, Lesbian, Transgender, and Supporters Alliance (BGLTSA) were offended that Pinkett Smith's comments seemed specific to heterosexual relationships. Conceding that there was nothing in her remarks that were remotely homophobic, the BGLTSA nonetheless expressed concern that her content was "extremely heteronormative"—meaning her comments implied that standard sexual relationships are only between males and females, making BGLTSA members feel uncomfortable.

The BGLTSA called for and received an apology from the Foundation, which is committed to "take responsibility to inform future speakers that they will be speaking to an audience diverse in race, ethnicity, religion, sexuality, gender and class."

In our day, voices daring to espouse traditional values, much less Christian ones, will be increasingly pressured to remain silent. They will not simply be met with hostility or be trivialized. There is increasing pressure for such voices never to be heard.

This highlights the Christian call to embody one of the more foundational character traits lauded in Scripture: courage. Many years ago the late Brent Curtis gave life-changing advice to author John Eldredge: "Let people feel the weight of who you are," he said, "and let them deal with it."

As pressure bears down on voices that would speak winsomely and compellingly into the cultural wasteland in ways that challenge the prevailing ethos, we must take heart in Christ and let people feel the weight of who we are in him, and let them deal with it.

And they will.

A performer in the Cultural Rhythms show who watched Pinkett Smith's speech said he thought the speech was "insightful." "You can never appeal to every single group," he said. "You'll always in some way be exclusive. I thought her message was clear. I thought it was sincere."

In other words, he listened. But first, someone had to stand up and speak.

So we end with a prayer, first offered by John R. W. Stott at the end of his short but profound book *Your Mind Matters:*

> I pray earnestly that God will raise up today a new generation of Christian apologists or Christian communicators, who will combine an absolute loyalty to the biblical gospel and an unwavering confidence in the power of the Spirit with a deep and sensitive understanding of the contemporary alternatives to the gospel; who will relate the one to the other with freshness, pungency, authority and relevance; and who will use their minds to reach other minds for Christ.

Appendix I

Three Book Lists

*M*any excellent reading lists have been compiled. For the Great Books, it would be difficult to improve on the collection brought together by Robert Maynard Hutchins and Mortimer Adler in *The Great Books of the Western World*.

Excellent introductions to the reading involved with a classical education can be found in Susan Wise Bauer's *The Well Educated Mind* as well as the collaborative effort of Louise Cowan and Os Guinness in their *Invitation to the Classics*. For a rigorous, academic list, see Brian J. Walsh and J. Richard Middleton's effort last updated in James Sire's *Discipleship of the Mind*.

Here I offer three different lists. The first consists of ten books that will give anyone's mind a good, solid start. If you haven't read one or more of these, start there. They are, by nature, popular introductions that offer a great deal of knowledge and facilitate learning. That is their strength. Very brief descriptions accompany these books.

The second list includes twenty-five books designed specifically to help form a Christian worldview, and most speak directly to that subject.

The third, and most demanding, list will introduce you to the "great conversation" through the Great Books. These selections represent a wide range of perspectives, both Christian and non-Christian. They are presented in roughly chronological order. This list is not meant to provide a complete education—you will quickly notice that books on science and mathematics, for example, have been omitted—but they provide a foundation for engaging the great ideas across time.

The first list can be read in fairly short order—the second list, from which you can pick and choose (I do not recommend reading them all), can be effectively perused in less than a year. The third list will occupy a bit more time, but at around 150 volumes it is within easy reach of most. Consider it a lifetime goal.

TEN TO START

Adler, Mortimer. *How to Read a Book.* A primer on how to read various types of books, including the skills involved in reading a book at the level it deserves.

Brown, Colin. *Philosophy and the Christian Faith.* An introduction to the principal philosophers and their ideas.

Lewis, C. S. *Mere Christianity.* A classic explanation of, and apologetic for, orthodox Christianity.

Niebuhr, H. Richard. *Christ and Culture.* A classic discussion of the five options for engaging the culture for Christ.

Noll, Mark A. *Turning Points.* Essays on the twelve turning points in Christian history.

Packer, J. I. *Knowing God.* A foundational theology on the doctrine of God.

Sayers, Dorothy. *The Mind of the Maker.* An example of a Christian worldview in full application.

Schaeffer, Francis. *Escape from Reason.* Schaeffer's seminal work on the reasons for the demise of Western thought.

Sire, James. *The Universe Next Door.* A classic overview of the dominant worldviews, such as existentialism, pantheism, postmodernism and naturalism.

Stott, John R. W. *Basic Christianity.* A foundational theology on the doctrine of Christ's person and work.

TWENTY-FIVE BOOKS TOWARD A CHRISTIAN WORLDVIEW

Bauer, Susan Wise. *The Well-Educated Mind.*
Blamires, Harry. *The Christian Mind.*
Bonhoeffer, Dietrich. *The Cost of Discipleship.*
Chesterton, G. K. *Orthodoxy.*
Colson, Charles. *How Now Shall We Live?*
Dawson, Christopher. *Religion and the Rise of Western Culture.*
Dooyeweerd, Herman. *Roots of Western Culture.*
Herrick, James A. *The Making of the New Spirituality.*
Holmes, Arthur. *All Truth Is God's Truth.*
Lewis, C. S. *The Abolition of Man.*
Meilaender, Gilbert. *Bioethics: A Primer for Christians.*
Moreland, J. P. *Love Your God with All Your Mind.*
Neuhaus, Richard John. *The Naked Public Square.*
Newbigin, Lesslie. *The Gospel in a Pluralist Society.*
Nicoli, Armand. *The Question of God.*
Noll, Mark A. *The Scandal of the Evangelical Mind.*
Pearcey, Nancy. *Total Truth.*
Schaeffer, Francis. *The God Who Is There.*
Sider, Ron. *Rich Christians in An Age of Hunger.*
ten Boom, Corrie. *The Hiding Place.*
Veith, Gene Edward. *Postmodern Times.*
Walsh, Brian J., and J. Richard Middleton. *The Transforming Vision.*
Weaver, Richard. *Ideas Have Consequences.*

White, James Emery. *Serious Times.*
Yancey, Philip. *What's So Amazing About Grace?*

ENTERING THE GREAT CONVERSATION[††]

The Epic of Gilgamesh.
Homer. *The Iliad; The Odyssey.*
Aeschylus. *Agamemnon; Choephoroe; Eumenides (The Oresteia).*
Sophocles. *Oedipus the King.*
Euripides. *Medea; The Bachantes.*
Aristophanes. *The Clouds; The Wasps; The Birds; The Frogs; The Lysistrata.*
Herodotus. *The History* ("History of the Persian Wars" or simply "The Histories").
Thucydides. *The History of the Peloponnesian War.*
Plato. *The Republic.*
Aristotle. *Nicomachean Ethics; On Poetics.*
Virgil. *The Eclogues; The Georges; The Aeneid.*
Plutarch. *The Lives of the Noble Grecians and Romans.*
Tacitus. *The Annals; The Histories.*
Augustine. *The Confessions; The City of God.*
Beowulf.
Thomas Aquinas. *Summa Theologica.*
Dante Alighieri. *The Divine Comedy.*
Sir Gawain and the Green Knight.
Geoffrey Chaucer. *The Canterbury Tales.*
The Second Shepherd's Play and *Everyman.*
Thomas More. *Utopia.*
Martin Luther. *The Babylonian Captivity of the Church; The Small Catechism.*
Bede. *The Ecclesiastical History of the English People.*

[††]Authors and titles listed chronologically.

Niccolo Machiavelli. *The Prince*.

John Calvin. *Institutes of the Christian Religion*.

Thomas Hobbes. *Leviathan*.

Michel de Montaigne. *Essays*.

William Shakespeare. *The Tragedy of King Richard the Third; A Midsummer-Night's Dream; Hamlet; The Tempest*.

John Donne. *Poems*.

George Herbert. *The Temple*.

Miguel de Cervantes. *The History of Don Quixote de la Mancha*.

René Descartes. *Meditations on First Philosophy; Objections Against the Meditations and Replies*.

Benedict de Spinoza. *Ethics*.

John Milton. *Paradise Lost*.

William Blake. *Songs of Innocence and of Experience*.

Blaise Pascal. *Pensées*.

John Bunyan. *The Pilgrim's Progress; Grace Abounding to the Chief of Sinners*.

John Locke. *A Letter Concerning Toleration; Concerning Civil Government* (second essay).

George Berkeley. *The Principles of Human Knowledge*.

David Hume. *An Enquiry Concerning Human Understanding*.

Jonathan Swift. *Gulliver's Travels*.

Jonathan Edwards. *A Treatise Concerning Religious Affections*.

Henry Fielding. *The History of Tom Jones; A Foundling*.

Montesquieu. *The Spirit of Laws*.

Jean Jacques Rousseau. *The Social Contract; Confessions*.

Adam Smith. *An Enquiry into the Nature and Causes of the Wealth of Nations*.

Edward Gibbon. *The Decline and Fall of the Roman Empire*.

Immanuel Kant. *The Critique of Pure Reason; The Critique of Practical Reason; The Critique of Judgment*.

Thomas Paine. *Common Sense*.

American State Papers; The Declaration of Independence; Articles of
    Confederation; The Constitution of the United States of America.
Alexander Hamilton, James Madison and John Jay. *The Federalist Papers.*
John Stuart Mill. *On Liberty; Representative Government; Utilitarianism.*
James Boswell. *The Life of Samuel Johnson.*
Georg W. F. Hegel. *The Philosophy of Right; The Philosophy of History.*
Jane Austen. *Pride and Prejudice.*
Mary Shelley. *Frankenstein.*
Johann Wolfgang von Goethe. *Faust.*
Alexis de Tocqueville. *Democracy in America.*
John Henry Newman. *Apologia Pro Vita Sua.*
Søren Kierkegaard. *Fear and Trembling.*
Charlotte Brontë. *Jane Eyre.*
Emily Brontë. *Wuthering Heights.*
John Keats. *The Great Odes.*
Henry David Thoreau. *Walden.*
William Wordsworth and Samuel Taylor Coleridge. *Lyrical Ballads.*
Ralph Waldo Emerson. *Essays.*
Frederick Douglas. *Narrative of the Life of Frederick Douglas: An American
    Slave.*
Nathaniel Hawthorne. *The Scarlet Letter.*
Karl Marx and Friedrich Engels. *Manifesto of the Communist Party.*
Karl Marx. *Capital.*
Herman Melville. *Moby Dick.*
Harriet Beecher Stowe. *Uncle Tom's Cabin.*
Gustave Flaubert. *Madame Bovary.*
Charles Darwin. *The Origin of Species by Means of Natural Selection.*
Emily Dickinson. *The Complete Poems.*
Charles Dickens. *Great Expectations; Oliver Twist.*
George Eliot. *Middlemarch.*

Gerard Manley Hopkins. *Poems.*

Leo Tolstoy. *War and Peace; Anna Karenina.*

Thomas Hardy. *The Return of the Native.*

Fyodor Dostoevsky. *The Brothers Karamazov.*

Henrik Ibsen. *A Doll's House.*

Henry James. *The Portrait of a Lady.*

Mark Twain. *The Adventures of Huckleberry Finn.*

Friedrich Nietzsche. *Twilight of the Idols.*

William James. *The Principles of Psychology.*

Oscar Wilde. *The Importance of Being Earnest.*

William Butler Yeats. *Poems.*

Max Weber. *The Protestant Ethic and the Spirit of Capitalism.*

Sigmund Freud. *The Interpretations of Dreams; Civilization and Its Discontents.*

Joseph Conrad. *Heart of Darkness.*

Anton Chekhov. *The Cherry Orchard.*

James Joyce. *Dubliners.*

George Bernard Shaw. *Saint Joan.*

F. Scott Fitzgerald. *The Great Gatsby.*

Adolph Hitler. *Mein Kampf.*

Virginia Woolf. *To the Lighthouse.*

Mohandas Gandhi. *An Autobiography: The Story of My Experiments with Truth.*

Robert Frost. *Poems.*

Aldous Huxley. *Brave New World.*

Franz Kafka. *The Trial.*

Thornton Wilder. *Our Town.*

Albert Camus. *The Stranger.*

William Faulkner. *Go Down, Moses.*

T. S. Eliot. *Four Quartets; Murder in the Cathedral.*

Jean Paul Sartre. *No Exit.*

Tennessee Williams. *A Streetcar Named Desire.*

Thomas Merton. *The Seven Storey Mountain.*

George Orwell. *1984.*

Alan Paton. *Cry, The Beloved Country.*

Arthur Miller. *Death of a Salesman.*

Samuel Beckett. *Waiting for Godot.*

Simone Weil. *Waiting for God.*

Dietrich Bonhoeffer. *Letters and Papers from Prison.*

Ralph Ellison. *Invisible Man.*

Dorothy Sayers. *The Mind of the Maker.*

C. S. Lewis. *The Screwtape Letters; Mere Christianity;* The Chronicles of Narnia; *Surprised by Joy; The Abolition of Man.*

J. R. R. Tolkien. *The Lord of the Rings.*

Eli Wiesel. *Night.*

Flannery O'Connor. *A Good Man Is Hard to Find.*

Eugene O'Neil. *Long Day's Journey into Night.*

Martin Luther King Jr. *Why We Can't Wait.*

Aleksandr Solzhenitsyn. *A Day in the Life of Ivan Denisovich; The Gulag Archipelago.*

Annie Dillard. *Pilgrim at Tinker Creek.*

Alex Haley. *Roots.*

Toni Morrison. *Beloved.*

Appendix 2

Resources for Learning

*T*here are numerous resources for learning as well as means of learning. The following short list of resources is meant to be introductory, but it should serve anyone interested in exploring the many ways we have to continue our learning for a lifetime.

AUDIO RESOURCES

The Teaching Company <www.teach12.com>. The Teaching Company is unique in that it tapes, for a wider, general audience, the best university lecturers teaching their most popular classes in their fields of specialty. As a result, the worlds of Harvard and Yale, Princeton and Duke, and Stanford and Georgetown become open to all with a willing mind. Though you should not expect the courses to be taught from an explicit acknowledgment of, much less an allegiance to, a Christian worldview, the vast majority of courses are fair, balanced and sensitive to diverse viewpoints.

Mars Hill Audio Journal <www.marshillaudio.org>. This bimonthly audio resource offers interviews and critiques in an impressive range of cultural engagements (art, music, poetry, film). Though not without its editorial biases, Mars Hill consistently offers thoughtful and engaging conversations that stimulate the mind.

LEARNING CENTERS

Gordon-Conwell Theological Seminary <www.gcts.edu>. There are many Christian seminaries that offer superb learning opportunities. I highlight Gordon-Conwell for several reasons: it is nondenominational, solidly evangelical in its moorings, one of the largest seminaries in the nation and has historically led the way in providing the best in a classical Christian education. Through its multiple campuses throughout the United States, its Semlink program and its other learning opportunities, it is one of the more accessible seminaries in the United States.

The Centurions Program <www.pfm.org>. There are many short-term programs offered by various organizations that are designed to develop a biblical worldview. One of the best is the Centurions Program, started by Charles Colson. Colson's goal is "to help Christians approach life with a biblical worldview so that they can in turn shape culture from a biblical perspective." The Centurions Program is an intensive, in-depth distance learning program that lasts one year. It involves daily devotionals, a rigorous reading program, homework assignments, three weekend residences (in Lansdowne, Virginia), meeting regularly with an accountability partner and a prayer partner, developing and teaching a worldview class, and participation in Web conferences and an online community.

WEBSITES

The Barna Group <www.barna.org>. Under the leadership of George Barna, the Barna Group consistently offers the latest and best societal snapshots through their wide-ranging research.

Christianity Today International <www.christianitytoday.com>. Christianity Today International is the umbrella organization for a number of first-rate periodicals, including such magazines as *Christianity Today* and *Books & Culture*. Its website not only provides access to a database of articles from such periodicals but also offers one of the best daily weblogs for news and information of interest to Christians. Their film forum, providing the latest in film reviews, is also superb.

C. S. Lewis Foundation <www.cslewis.org>. While a number of sites are devoted to Lewis, this is the official site of the C. S. Lewis Foundation, which also oversees The Kilns (Lewis's home). The foundation provides numerous conferences and learning opportunities, including the biannual Oxbridge conference.

Emerging Scholars Network <www.emergingscholars.org>. An enterprise of InterVarsity Christian Fellowship, the Emerging Scholars Network aims to "identify, encourage and support the next generation of Christian scholars, at all stages of their academic careers, who will be a redeeming influence in higher education."

Focus on the Family <www.family.org>. The home site of James Dobson's *Focus on the Family* offers a portal to a number of helpful resources regarding family, public policy and culture.

First Things <www.firstthings.com>. This website for one of the more thoughtful journals on religion and culture, *First Things,* provides search access to a database of past articles.

London Institute for Contemporary Christianity <www.licc.org.uk>. Founded by John Stott, the London Institute for Contemporary Christianity equips Christians to make a difference in such areas as work, culture, media and communication. This website offers a number of helpful resources as well as study programs.

Serious Times <www.serioustimes.com>. This website offers numerous resources for learning, including downloadable whitepapers on key issues, audio tapes, books, homeschooling resources, links and the ability to subscribe to the biweekly *Serious Times Update.*

PERIODICALS

The Atlantic Monthly <www.theatlantic.com>. "This general editorial magazine focuses on contemporary social and cultural issues. Its emphasis includes a wide variety of subjects. The *Atlantic Monthly* encourages a rich and balanced lifestyle through commentary, criticism, fiction and humor" (from the publisher). Published monthly.

The New York Times Book Review <www.nytimes.com/pages/books/index.html>. The premiere collection of reviews for new books, definitive bestseller lists and ads for new releases of interest. Published weekly.

Books & Culture <www.booksandculture.com>. One of the most thoughtful, well-edited new Christian publications. This bimonthly review focuses on new books but also covers film, personalities and more. Books are often brought together under varying themes, creating insightful bibliographic essays.

Christianity Today <www.christianitytoday.com>. Founded in 1956 by Billy Graham and calling itself "A Magazine of Evangelical Conviction," *Christianity Today* is undoubtedly the leading feature and news periodical of evangelical Christianity. Published monthly.

First Things <www.firstthings.com>. A journal of religion, culture and public life, *First Things* is shaped by Richard John Neuhaus and has become one of the more influential Christian journals of the day. It is published by the Institute on Religion and Public Life, "an interreligious, nonpartisan research and education institute whose purpose is to advance a religiously informed public philosophy for the ordering of society." Published monthly.

Harper's Magazine <www.harpers.org>. Founded in 1850 and continuously published ever since, *Harper's Magazine* is home not only to the famed "Harper's Index" (a collection of facts designed to bemuse) but also to thoughtful essays, readings from various sources, photo essays, stories and, of course, reviews. In its own words, it is "an American journal of literature, politics, culture, and the arts." Published monthly.

The Hedgehog Review <www.virginia.edu/iasc/hedgehog.html?> As self-described, "*The Hedgehog Review* is an interdisciplinary, academic journal of critical reflections on contemporary culture, published three times a year by the Institute for Advanced Studies in Culture. Each issue addresses a single theme with articles, interviews, book reviews, and an annotated bibliography written by leading scholars from throughout the disciplines." Edited by James Davison Hunter, this is one of the more thoughtful journals on culture in publication.

The Times Literary Supplement <www.the-tls.co.uk>. The British counterpart to the *New York Times Book Review.* It promises to provide "comprehensive weekly coverage of the latest and most important publications, in every subject, in several languages—AND current theater, opera, exhibitions, and film." Published weekly.

Touchstone <www.touchstonemag.com>. Referring to itself as "A Journal of Mere Christianity," *Touchstone* openly admits its love affair with all things "inkling." Published by The Fellowship of St. James, *Touchstone* advertises itself as a "Christian journal, conservative in doctrine and eclectic in content, with editors and readers from each of the three great divisions of Christendom—Protestant, Catholic, and Orthodox." Its essays are among the most thoughtful in print, with a heart for sanctity of life issues and the suffering church. Published monthly.

The Week <www.theweekmagazine.com>. Boasting "All you need to know about everything that matters," *The Week* is a unique periodical in that it provides a summary of American and international media reports. Rather than offer its own reports, it summarizes what everyone else is reporting, revealing the many perspectives that abound. It describes itself as "a witty, informative, important, and completely indispensable digest of the best reporting and writing from the U.S. and international press. In just 40 pages, it will bring you up to date on what's happening at home and abroad, and what the experts are saying about it." Published weekly.

World <www.worldmag.com>. One of the more conservative periodicals in evangelicalism, *World* positions itself as a Christian alternative to, say, *Newsweek* or *U.S. News & World Report*. Its mission statement: "To report, interpret, and illustrate the news in a timely, accurate, enjoyable, and arresting fashion from a perspective committed to the Bible as the inerrant Word of God." Published weekly.

Notes

Introduction: A Mind for God

page 10   "a study of faculty members at U.S. colleges and universities":
Stanley Rothman, S. Robert Lichter and Neil Nevitte, "Politics
and Professional Advancement Among College Faculty," *The Forum* 1067 (2005): 7. Accessed at <www.cmpa.com/documents/
05.03.29.Forum.Survey.pdf>.

page 10   The director of the National Center for Science Education's response to intelligent design: Cited in Greg Toppo, "Kansas
Schools Can Teach 'Intelligent Design,' " *USA Today,* November
9, 2005, p. 7D.

pages 10-11 "the ever-increasing number of college professors": Charles Colson, "Money Talks," *BreakPoint,* October 12, 2005. Accessible at
<www.pfm.org>.

page 12   "Ireland had one moment of unblemished glory": Thomas Cahill, *How the Irish Saved Civilization* (New York: Doubleday,
1995), p. 3.

page 12   "when Islam began its medieval expansion": Cahill, *How the
Irish Saved Civilization,* pp. 193-94.

page 13   "starting point for the conquest of the world": Alister McGrath,
The Twilight of Atheism (New York: Doubleday, 2004), p. xi.

page 13   "We may talk of 'conquering'": John Stott, *Your Mind Matters*
(Downers Grove, Ill.: InterVarsity Press, 1972), p. 13.

page 14   Hofstadter on American anti-intellectualism: See Richard Hof-
                 stadter, *Anti-Intellectualism in American Life* (New York: Vintage,
                 1962), pp. 55-80; see also Mark Noll's interaction with Hof-
                 stadter's contention in *The Scandal of the Evangelical Mind*
                 (Grand Rapids: Eerdmans, 1994), pp. 11-12.

page 14   "What indeed has Athens to do with Jerusalem?": Tertullian *On
                 the Proscription of Heretics* 6, *The Ante-Nicene Fathers,* ed. Alex-
                 ander Roberts and James Donaldson (Peabody, Mass.: Hen-
                 drickson, 1999), 3:246.

page 15   "There is no longer a Christian mind": Harry Blamires, *The
                 Christian Mind: How Should a Christian Think?* (Ann Arbor,
                 Mich.: Servant Books, 1978).

page 16   "If evangelicals do not take seriously the larger world of the in-
                 tellect": Noll, *Scandal of the Evangelical Mind,* p. 34.

Chapter 1: The Christian Mind

page 19   National Study of Youth and Religion: Christian Smith, *Soul
                 Searching: The Religious and Spiritual Lives of American Teenagers*
                 (Oxford: Oxford University Press, 2005), p. 171.

page 20   Moralistic Therapeutic Deism: Smith, *Soul Searching,* p. 165.

pages 20-21   Os Guinness on Christian thinking: Os Guinness, *Fit Bodies, Fat
                 Minds* (Grand Rapids: Baker, 1994), p. 136.

page 22   Flannery O'Connor as a "Christian Realist": See Robert Ellsberg,
                 ed., *Flannery O'Connor: Spiritual Writings* (Maryknoll, N.Y.: Or-
                 bis, 2003), p. 49.

page 22   "It makes a great difference to the look of a novel": Flannery
                 O'Connor, "Novelist and Believer" (1963), cited in ibid., p. 68.

Chapter 2: The Cultural Mind

page 25   Weikart on Darwinism and the Nazis: Richard Weikart, *From
                 Darwin to Hitler: Evolutionary Ethics, Eugenics, and Racism in Ger-
                 many* (New York: Palgrave Macmillan, 2004).

pages 25-26   This is what Richard Weaver: Richard Weaver, *Ideas Have Con-*

sequences (Chicago: University of Chicago Press, 1948).

page 26   Solzhenitsyn's country's spiritual demise: Aleksandr Solzhenitsyn, from his acceptance speech for the Templeton Prize for
Progress in Religion, cited by Carl F. H. Henry, *The Christian
Mindset in a Secular Society* (Portland, Ore.: Multnomah, 1978),
p. 94.

page 26   Many Jews and Christians are secularists: David Klinghoffer,
"That Other Church," *Christianity Today,* January 2005, p. 62.

page 27   "relatively thin on the ground": Peter Berger, *The Deseculariza-
tion of the World* (Grand Rapids: Eerdmans, 1999), p. 10.

page 27   "America is a land of Indians ruled by Swedes": See Huston
Smith, *Why Religion Matters* (San Francisco: HarperSanFran-
cisco, 2002), p. 103.

page 27   "the new pope is not driven by polls": See Joseph Ratzinger, *Salt
of the Earth: Christianity and the Catholic Church at the End of the
Millenium,* trans. Adrian Walker (San Francisco: Ignatius,
1997).

page 28   "We are moving toward": David Yount, "Christians Must Keep
God's Rule, New Pope Reminds Us," *The (Tacoma, Washington)
News Tribune,* April 25, 2005.

page 29   Allan Bloom reflects on his role as a university educator: Allan
Bloom, *The Closing of the American Mind: How Higher Education
Has Failed Democracy and Impoverished the Souls of Today's Stu-
dents* (New York: Simon & Schuster, 1987), p. 25.

page 29   "God is not a proper topic for conversation": Page Smith, *Killing
the Spirit: Higher Education in America* (New York: Viking, 1990),
p. 5.

page 30   Christianity and Enlightenment intellectuals: Harold A. Net-
land, *Dissonant Voices: Religious Pluralism and the Question of
Truth* (Grand Rapids: Eerdmans, 1991), p. 30.

page 30   "The true believer is the real danger": Bloom, *Closing of the
American Mind,* p. 26.

page 31   "Man is the being whose project is to be God": Jean Paul Sartre,

Existentialism and Human Emotions (New York: Citadel Press, 1957), p. 63.

page 31   "the culture of narcissism": Christopher Lasch, *The Culture of Narcissism* (New York: W. W. Norton, 1991), p. 7.

page 32   "I believe what I can understand": Stanley J. Grenz, *A Primer on Postmodernism* (Grand Rapids: Eerdmans, 1996), p. 62.

page 32   "Age of science": Gerard Piel, *The Age of Science: What Scientists Learned in the Twentieth Century* (New York: Basic Books, 2001).

page 32   "it is not simply unknowable but meaningless": For an informed critique of many of the more popular aspects of applied naturalism, see Phillip E. Johnson, *Reason in the Balance: The Case Against Naturalism in Science, Law and Education* (Downers Grove, Ill.: InterVarsity Press, 1995).

page 33   "the goal is to rid ourselves of a 'demon-haunted' world": Carl Sagan, *The Demon-Haunted World: Science as a Candle in the Dark* (New York: Random House, 1995).

Chapter 3: The Library as Armory

page 37   "Our library is our armory": Monk cited by Daniel J. Boorstin, *The Discoverers: A History of Man's Search to Know His World and Himself* (New York: Random House, 1983), p. 492.

page 37   "Reading at Risk" report: "Reading at Risk: A Survey of Literary Reading in America," Research Division Report 42 (2002), National Endowment of the Arts. The study was based on over 17,000 adults covering most major demographic groups and conducted by the U.S. Bureau of the Census and spanning twenty years of polling.

page 39   "you must read seriously: history, theology, politics": Susan Wise Bauer, *The Well-Educated Mind: A Guide to the Classical Education You Never Had* (New York: W. W. Norton, 2003), p. 25.

page 40   "Only 100 hours were spent reading": *New York Times,* August 24, 1997, cited in *The Pastor's Weekly Briefing* 5, no. 35 (1997): 2.

pages 40-41   George Orwell and Aldous Huxley on books: Neil Postman, *Amusing Ourselves to Death* (New York: Penguin, 1985), p. vii.

page 42   "If a man wants to read good books": Arthur Schopenhauer, *Some Forms of Literature,* cited by Mortimer Adler and Charles Van Doren, *Great Treasury of Western Thought* (New York: R. R. Bowker, 1977), p. 1021.

page 42   "Richard Weaver observes that it may be doubted": Richard M. Weaver, *Ideas Have Consequences* (Chicago: University of Chicago Press, 1984), p. 14.

page 43   "the road to education lay through the great books": Robert Maynard Hutchins, *The Great Conversation: The Substance of a Liberal Education,* Great Books of the Western World (Chicago: Encyclopaedia Britannica, 1952), 1:xi.

page 43   "And what are the great books?": Ibid., p. xi.

page 43   "the 'old' books": C. S. Lewis, "On the Reading of Old Books," in *God in the Dock: Essays on Theology and Ethics,* ed. Walter Hooper (Grand Rapids: Eerdmans, 1970), pp. 200-207.

pages 43-44   The "Great Books": Published by Encyclopaedia Britannica and the University of Chicago, the fifty-four volumes were simply called the "Great Books of the Western World." It has since been updated to include such modern luminaries as Kafka, Barth, Wittgenstein, Einstein, Proust, Heidegger and Weber.

page 45   Descartes on reading great books: René Descartes, "Discourse on Method" 1, *The Essential Descartes,* ed. Margaret D. Wilson (New York: Meridian/New American Library, 1969), p. 109.

page 45   "Every age has its own outlook": Lewis, "Reading of Old Books," p. 202.

page 46   "The Christian is prepared to say": N. T. Wright, cited by Tim Stafford in "New Theologians," *Christianity Today,* February 8, 1999, p. 45.

pages 47-48   The story of Augustine's conversion: Adapted from Charles Colson, *Loving God* (Grand Rapids: Zondervan, 1983), pp. 45-53.

page 49   "If I were the devil": J. I. Packer, foreword to R. C. Sproul, *Know-*

ing Scripture (Downers Grove, Ill.: InterVarsity Press, 1977), pp. 7-10.

Chapter 4: The Lost Tools of Learning

page 52   "endless volleys of nonsense": Quentin J. Schultze, *Habits of the High-Tech Heart: Living Virtuously in the Information Age* (Grand Rapids: Baker, 2002), p. 21.

page 52   "the 'Daily Me'": See Cass Sunstein, *Republic.Com* (Princeton, N.J.: Princeton University Press, 2001).

page 53   The "threefold way" and the "fourfold way": See Ralph M. Mc-Inerny, *A Student's Guide to Philosophy* (Wilmington, Del.: ISI Books, 1999), pp. 18-19.

page 53   "decisive for the development of a Christian mind": This is the spirit behind many who choose to homeschool their children. See Jessie Wise and Susan Wise Bauer, *The Well-Trained Mind: A Guide to Classical Education at Home* (New York: W. W. Norton, 1999). The Wises returned to the ancient *trivium* for intellectual formation.

page 53   "T. S. Eliot wrote of the tragedy": T. S. Eliot, *Christianity and Culture* (New York: Harcourt Brace, 1948), p. 175.

page 55   "The point of an education": Clifford Williams, *The Life of the Mind: A Christian Perspective* (Grand Rapids: Baker, 2002), pp. 28-29

page 55   "It is a good life": Ibid., p. 41.

pages 55-56 "six thousand names, phrases, dates and concepts": E. D. Hirsch Jr., Joseph F. Kett and James Trefil, *The New Dictionary of Cultural Literacy,* 3rd ed. (New York: Houghton Mifflin, 2002).

page 56   "*Christian* literacy": See Jo H. Lewis and Gordon A. Palmer, *What Every Christian Should Know* (Wheaton, Ill.: Victor, 1989).

page 58   Twelve seminal events of Christian history: Mark Noll, *Turning Points: Decisive Moments in the History of Christianity* (Grand Rapids: Baker, 1997).

page 62   Brooklyn College professor's online essay: Timothy Shortell,

"Religion and Morality: A Contradiction Explained," *The Anti-Naturals* <www.anti-naturals.org/theory/religion.html>.

page 63   "I would like to see professors in high positions": Jacob Gersh-man, "Professor Who Belittled Believers Drops Bid to Head Up a Department," *The New York Sun,* June 8, 2005 <www.nysyn .com>; "Top Prof Sparks Outrage," *New York Daily News,* May 23, 2005 <www.nydailynews.com>; Shoshana Baum, "Anti-Religion Prof's Promotion Rankles Brooklyn Campus," *Jewish Week,* June 3, 2005 <www.thejewishweek.com>.

page 63   "contemporary university culture is hollow at its core": George Marsden, *The Outrageous Idea of Christian Scholarship* (New York: Oxford University Press, 1997), p. 3.

page 63   "priests who have lost their faith, and kept their jobs": Kelly Monroe, ed., *Finding God at Harvard: Spiritual Journeys of Think-ing Christians* (Grand Rapids: Zondervan, 1996), p. 15.

page 63   "even Christians scholars have not reflected much": For an ex-cellent example of what this might look like, consider *Shaping a Christian Worldview: The Foundations of Christian Higher Educa-tion*, ed. David S. Dockery and Gregory Alan Thornbury (Nash-ville: Broadman & Holman, 2002).

Chapter 5: Sacred Thinking

page 65   "philosophers no longer wrestle with the big questions": See Ralph M. McInerny, *A Student's Guide to Philosophy* (Wilmington, Del.: ISI Books, 1999), pp. 10-11.

page 66   Malcolm Gladwell's "blink": Malcolm Gladwell, *Blink: The Power of Thinking Without Thinking* (New York: Little, Brown, 2005).

page 66   "one half of the world is asking advice of the other half": Henri J. M. Nouwen, *Reaching Out: The Three Movements of the Spiritual Life* (New York: Doubleday, 1976), p. 39.

page 68   "these are euphemisms for a worldview": Christian Smith, *Soul Searching* (Oxford: Oxford University Press, 2005), pp. 176-77.

page 69   "paganism holds all the most valuable advertising space": T. S.

Eliot, *Christianity and Culture* (New York: Harcourt Brace, 1976), p. 18.

page 69   ABC news story on the death of Princess Diana: "Some Perspective, Please," *World,* September 20, 1997, p. 9.

page 70   Parents Television Council on MTV: David Bauder, "Group Blasts MTV for 'Sleazy' Shows," *Charlotte Observer,* Saturday, February 5, 2005, p. 4E.

pages 70-71   Kaiser Family Foundation study of sex on TV: Ann Oldenburg, "Turning on TV; More of a Turn-On?" *USA Today,* November 10, 2005, p. 1D.

page 71   "If characters are portrayed as having intercourse": Ibid.

page 71   "films and television tell us the way we conduct our lives": George Lucas, cited by Michael Medved, *Hollywood vs. America* (New York: HarperCollins, 1992), p. 271.

page 71   "films should not be the end-all for what is true": Oliver Stone, cited in "Oliver Stone: Forget Facts; Films Aren't About Accuracy," *Charlotte Observer,* September 23, 1997, p. 2A.

page 71   "the object of opening the mind": G. K. Chesterton, *Essential Writings,* ed. William Griffin (Maryknoll, N.Y.: Orbis, 2003), p. 63.

page 71   A "speeded-up mind": Neil Postman, *The Disappearance of Childhood* (New York: Vintage, 1994), p. 116.

page 71   "We live forward, but we can only think backward": Søren Kierkegaard, cited by John Lukacs, *A Student's Guide to the Study of History,* ISI Guides to the Major Disciplines (Wilmington, Del.: ISI Books, 2000), p. 3.

page 73   "such differences might look like mere partisanship": George Marsden, *The Outrageous Idea of Christian Scholarship* (New York: Oxford University Press, 1997), p. 62.

page 73   "By an evangelical 'life of the mind' I mean": Mark Noll, *The Scandal of the Evangelical Mind* (Grand Rapids: Eerdmans, 1994), p. 7.

page 73   The concept of a worldview: On how *worldview* has been treated by a variety of thinkers, see David K. Naugle, *Worldview: The*

History of a Concept (Grand Rapids: Eerdmans, 2002).

page 74　　"a way to engage constructively the whole range of human expression": Gene Edward Veith, "Reading and Writing Worldviews," in *The Christian Imagination,* ed. Leland Ryken, rev. ed. (Colorado Springs: Shaw, 2002), p. 119.

page 74　　"the consistency and agreement of our ideas": Jonathan Edwards, "Notes on the Mind," in *The Works of Jonathan Edwards: Scientific and Philosophical Writings*, ed. Wallace E. Anderson (New Haven, Conn.: Yale University Press, 1980), pp. 341-42.

page 74　　the seven basic questions for any worldview: James W. Sire, *Discipleship of the Mind: Learning to Love God in the Ways We Think* (Downers Grove, Ill.: InterVarsity Press, 1990), pp. 30-31. The wording of Sire's questions have been slightly altered.

page 74　　Colson and Pearcey's worldview questions: Charles Colson and Nancy Pearcey, *How Now Shall We Live* (Wheaton, Ill.: Tyndale House, 1999), p. 14.

page 74　　"the discoverer of DNA": Francis Crick, *Life Itself* (New York: Simon & Schuster, 1981).

page 75　　"There are two types of law: just and unjust": Martin Luther King Jr., *Why We Can't Wait (Letter from a Birmingham Jail)* (New York: Mentor/New American Library, 1964), p. 82.

page 76　　"You can make all A's and still flunk life": Walker Percy, cited in Ralph C. Wood, *Contending for the Faith* (Waco, Tex.: Baylor University Press, 2003), p. 116.

pages 76-77　Chilling report about "The Lottery": Adapted from Os Guinness, *Time for Truth* (Grand Rapids: Baker, 2000), pp. 21-23.

Chapter 6: A Rule for the Mind

page 80　　"Every thoughtful person . . . has a rule": Thomas Moore, cited in *The Rule of St. Benedict,* ed. Timothy Fry (New York: Random House, 1998), p. xvi.

page 81　　Dallas Willard's definition of a spiritual discipline: Dallas Willard, *The Spirit of the Disciplines* (San Francisco: Harper & Row,

1988), p. 156.

page 81   "thinking Christianly is first and foremost a matter of love": Os
              Guinness, *Fit Bodies, Fat Minds* (Grand Rapids: Baker, 1994), p. 19.

page 83   "All you need are a shelf full of books": Susan Wise Bauer, *The
              Well-Educated Mind: A Guide to the Classical Education You Never
              Had* (New York: W. W. Norton, 2003), p. 15.

page 83   Bauer's suggestions for reading: Ibid., pp. 22-23.

page 84   "Some books are to be tasted": Francis Bacon, *Of Studies,* cited
              in Mortimer Adler and Charles Van Doren, *Great Treasury of
              Western Thought* (New York: R. R. Bowker, 1977), p. 1018.

page 84   "Can you spare one hour a day?": Will Durant, *The Greatest
              Minds and Ideas of All Time,* ed. and comp. John Little (New
              York: Simon & Schuster, 2002), p. 65.

page 86   "Go, sit in your cell": Abbot Moses, cited in Thomas Merton,
              *The Wisdom of the Desert: Sayings from the Desert Fathers of the
              Fourth Century* (New York: Sheldon Press, 1961), 13:30.

page 86   "Silence is the absence of sound": Frederick Buechner, *Whistling
              in the Dark* (San Francisco: Harper & Row, 1988), pp. 97-98.

Chapter 7: Thinking Out Loud

pages 89-90 "Ideas have consequences": George Weigel, *Letters to a Young
               Catholic* (New York: Basic Books, 2004), pp. 43-44.

page 90   "The study of . . . Christian thought": Robert Louis Wilken, *The
               Spirit of Early Christian Thought* (New Haven, Conn.: Yale Uni-
               versity Press, 2003), p. xiv.

pages 90-91 The fact and the significance of the resurrection: Thomas C. Oden,
               After Modernity . . . What? (Grand Rapids: Zondervan, 1990), p. 68.

pages 91-92 "A real spiritual life does exactly the opposite": Henri Nouwen,
               Reaching Out: The Three Movements of the Spiritual Life (New
               York: Doubleday, 1976), pp. 50-51.

page 92   Intellect and intelligence: Richard Hofstadter, *Anti-Intellectualism
               in American Life* (New York: Alfred A. Knopf, 1963), pp. 24-25.

page 93   "think about the strategies of justice and love": Dennis

Hollinger, *Head, Heart and Hands: Bringing Together Christian Thought, Passion and Action* (Downers Grove, Ill.: InterVarsity Press, 2005), p. 44.

page 94 "A believer's wisdom is found": See Jürgen Goetzmann, "Mind," *The New International Dictionary of New Testament Theology,* ed. Colin Brown (Grand Rapids: Zondervan, 1971), 2:616-20; see also Jürgen Goetzmann, Colin Brown and H. Weigel, "Wisdom, Folly, Philosophy," in *The New International Dictionary of New Testament Theology,* ed. Colin Brown (Grand Rapids: Zondervan, 1971), 3:1023-38.

page 94 "the *responsibility* of knowledge": Os Guinness, "Knowing Means Doing: A Challenge to Think Christianly," *Radix* 18, no. 1 (1987), as cited by James W. Sire in *Discipleship of the Mind* (Downers Grove, Ill.: InterVarsity Press, 1990), p. 23.

page 94 "a deliberate violation of the responsibility of knowledge": Os Guinness, *Fit Bodies, Fat Minds,* (Grand Rapids: Baker, 1994), p. 147.

page 94 Rousseau's child-rearing theories: Paul Johnson, *Intellectuals* (New York: Harper & Row, 1988), pp. 1-28.

page 97 Jada Pinkett Smith's Cultural Rhythms show address: See Evelyn Lilly, "Cultural Rhythms Showcases Talent," *Harvard Crimson,* Monday, February 28, 2005 <www.thecrimson.com>; Anna M. Friedman, "Pinkett Smith's Remarks Debated," *Harvard Crimson,* March 2, 2005 <www.thecrimson.com>.

page 98 "Let people feel the weight": John Eldredge, *Wild at Heart* (Grand Rapids: Zondervan, 2001), p. 149.

page 99 "A performer in the Cultural Rhythms show": Lilly, "Cultural Rhythms Showcase."

page 99 John Stott's prayer: John R. W. Stott, *Your Mind Matters* (Downers Grove, Ill.: InterVarsity Press, 1973), p. 52.

Appendix 1: Three Book Lists

page 101 Walsh and Middleton's academic list: For what they call "A Bibliography We Can't Live Without," see James W. Sire, *Disciple-ship of the Mind* (Downers Grove, Ill.: InterVarsity Press, 1990), pp. 219-43.

To learn more about seminars, audiotapes and other resources from James Emery White, visit the Serious Times website <www.serioustimes.com>. Serious Times is a ministry with the vision of transformed lives through the spiritual development of Christians' lives and the pursuit of a Christian mind. The website also includes information about the annual Serious Times Church and Culture Conference.